ARCHDIOCESE OF MILWAUKEE

P.O. Box 2018
Milwaukee, WI 53201

The Crisis of Au

Monsignor George A. Kelly

The Crisis of Authority

John Paul II
and the American Bishops

REGNERY GATEWAY

Nihil Obstat: James T. O'Connor, STD

Imprimatur: Joseph T. O'Keefe
             Vicar General, Archdiocese of New York

September 8, 1981

The *nihil obstat* and *imprimatur* are official declarations that a book or pamphlet is free of doctrinal or moral error. No implication is contained therein that those who have granted the nihil obstat and imprimatur agree with the contents, opinions or statements expressed.

Published 1982 by Regnery Gateway
360 West Superior Street
Chicago, Illinois 60610

International Standard Book Number: 0-89526-666-0
Library of Congress Card Catalogue Number: 81-52143

Manufactured in the United States of America

Contents

Preface

The thesis of this book is that the chief responsibility for the on-going difficulties of the Catholic Church in the United States now rests with the American bishops.

That was not always a demonstrable thesis. This writer's *The Battle for the American Church* (New York: Doubleday, 1979) suggested differently—that scholars and writers were mainly at fault. They were the ones who interpreted the documents of Vatican II in ways never intended by John XXIII and the Council Fathers. The same book indicated that, while the Catholic academics misused their new freedom to destroy the integrity of the Catholic community, the Catholic bishops sat on the sidelines. Other outsiders to the breakdown of Catholic order were the laity in the pews. Only once in the early post-conciliar period were they asked about what they wanted to change in their religious life. That was the parish by parish survey across the United States about the abolition of the six holy days, made shortly after the Council ended. The people said "no". During the pontificate of Paul VI there was no effort to interfere with experimentation, although as it progressed it was clear that the Pope was distressed by the irresponsibility of theologians, liturgists, religious superiors, social activists and by more than a few bishops.

It was obvious too, even before the end of the Council in 1965, that the radical reformers (Kung was only the best publicized), not satisfied with their gains in Vatican II, intended to dismantle the Catholic Church. Paul VI's signature was hardly affixed to Vatican II's sixteen constitutions and decrees when revisionists went to work on Catholic moral standards. Next came the effort to reduce the Catholic doctrinal commitment to many of the Church's traditional formulas.

During the years 1965-1978 what were bishops to do? They may have been the only major figures in the Church who took the Council seriously. They gave experimenters the leeway they needed, and the benefit of the doubt about their intentions. Furthermore, bishops chosen by Rome to supervise a peaceful Church were hardly skilled in the art of dealing with revolutionaries, which is what the dissidents in fact became. By the time of *Humanae Vitae*, Paul VI was disinclined by disposition, as by age, to counteract the force of his enemies with equal force. He was unable and unwilling to use the procedures of Catholic law to restrain those tearing apart the fabric of Catholic society.

The election of John Paul II to the papacy was not a happenstance. He was chosen by a College of Cardinals fully conscious of how far Catholic divisions had multiplied. From the beginning of his pontificate the new pope made clear that theologians and religious communities could not act irresponsibly and expect him to stand by in silence. His disciplinary moves against Hans Kung and rebellious Jesuits are only the more publicized elements of his program to restore a semblance of order to the Church. Secular media with the assistance from Catholic dissidents have caricatured his strong rule as the product of his narrow Polish background. Factually, this pope does what strong popes of any national background do when faced with widespread denials of Catholic doctrine. Catholic Church authority figures move more slowly against their enemies than their counterparts in civil society, but when the stakes are high they usually act effectively. And in this most recent case what was threatened by Catholic disorder was the renewal of Christian life, the updating of Catholic institutions, the evangelization of the unbelieving segment of the world's population, and the restoration of Christian unity, all part of the new directions proposed by Vatican II, and indeed the unity of the Catholic Church itself.

John Paul II has proved to be an activist pope. His first years involved preaching the Catholic gospels to five continents, and the issuance of three encyclicals, two of them critical documents on how Catholic catechism classes and Catholic universities should be run. He also directed the world's bishops to adhere strictly to Roman instructions on liturgy and the administration of sacraments and to uphold important Catholic moral standards. These were a new pope's efforts to improve the content and quality of Catholic life. However, John Paul realized that he could not succeed alone. Affirmative action by the entire hierarchy was necessary. The Jesuit Henri de Lubac in *The Splendour of the Church* (New York: Sheed and Ward, 1956, pp. 196-197) once stated a fundamental Catholic principle:

The Church is a community, but in order to be that community She is first a hierarchy. The Church which we call our Mother is not some ideal and unreal Church but this hierarchical Church herself; not the Church as we might dream her but the Church as she exists in fact, here and now.

There are those in places of high Church influence who no longer have confidence that the present American hierarchy can fulfill the expectations of their office. Others seeking radical change in Catholic doctrine are content with the present Catholic drift or have become convinced that the U.S. bishops, not the Pope, represent the wave of the Church's future. These latter credit former Apostolic Delegate Jean Jadot's episcopal appointments for the redirection of the American Church toward stress on the humanity of Christ and humanist goals rather than on the supernatural values traditionally associated with the Church.

The present difficulties of Catholicism may have their origins precisely in disagreements over just how much humanism the Church can afford. George Santayana thought that Catholicism stands or falls on its supernatural message:

"Its sole dignity lies there. It will not convert the world; it never did and it never could. It will remain a voice crying in the wilderness; but it will believe what it cries" (*Winds of Doctrine*,[New York: Dent, 1913], p. 56-57).

The basic elements of this supernatural message are the subject matter of the current argument in the Church. Doubts have been raised whether Christ ever called himself the Son of God, doubts about what he actually said, whether he founded a Church, established upon his apostles with the bishops as their successors, Mass as a Sacrifice or Peter as the primate as the Catholics say he was, whether today's Catholic insistence on doctrinal unity has any validity from a New Testament standpoint. Those speaking of a *Vatican Three Church* see in the making a new broadly based religious community, one whose central dogma after commitment to Jesus will be 'Fellowship'. In that Church the legalistic demands on believers will be fewer, and the stress on personal conversion will be greater. Involvement in humanizing the conditions under which the poor live and respect for confessional differences about gospel meanings will also be important characteristics. Although historic Catholicism is highly supernaturalistic, it is the humanistic component which will dominate the future Church.

While the *Vatican Three Church* is pictured as representing progress for Christianity, some would argue it really is reactionary because it denies the validity of what is distinctive of Catholicism, if not of Christianity itself. The lines of battle, therefore, may well be drawn between those who look upon old line orthodoxy as pre-scientific and anti-humanistic and those who insist that God's revelation to man was completed with Christ, that the Catholic Church is the special guardian of this revelation. Paul VI belonged to the second school. He saw the fundamental principle of Catholic faith to be the following:

> We can understand why the Catholic Church in the past and today has given and gives so much importance to the scrupulous presentation of the authentic revelation. She considers it an invaluable treasure and is sternly aware of her fundamental duty to defend and transmit the doctrine of the faith in unequivocal terms. Orthodoxy is her first concern. The pastoral magisterium is her primary and providential function (English *L'Osservatore Romano* 19 January 1972).

Vatican Three Church protagonists give little credit to Rome for those humanist trends which have always characterized Catholicism. In modern times it was the social and political encyclicals of modern popes, not the writings of theologians, which restated and deepened the Church's role in temporal matters. But this was never done at the expense of compromising the supernatural components of Christianity. In fact, it was the Church's claim to a divine foundation, and this alone, which justified the Church's intervention in the worldly affairs of men. Most of the Church's proclaimed social progressives, like Bishop Ketteler in Germany, Don Luigi Sturzo in Italy and Msgr. John A. Ryan in the United States, were orthodox believers in Catholicism's unique mission to men on behalf of Jesus Christ. That is, until recently. The present problem of the Church is that "progress for certain Catholics involves rejection of important Catholic doctrines.

Dissident theologians and some bishops do not wish to see the ongoing and open battle in the U.S. for control of Church definitions described in these terms. It looks too absolute, too ideological. They speak rather of partial compromises by the Church on revelation in the American mould — reduce the importance of Marian doctrines, identify papal primacy with honor and service rather than jurisdiction, encourage self-determination at the regional or continental level, especially in liturgical and moral choices, etc. On the surface a good theological case can be made for variations in a Church as large as the world's expanse of people and places. However, does failure to train children for first confession or downgrading private absolution for adults possibly suggest a denial of faith in need for the sacrament of penance? Does not the celebration of Mass with a "Eucharistic host" made of something other than bread or with grape juice raise questions whether the belief remains that Christ instituted the Eucharist as the Catholic Church understands this ritual? If believing Christians are free to use contraceptives for good reason, are they free to have an abortion, or to take a second spouse? The implication of an affirmative answer to these questions is that the Catholic Church is not a sure guide to the meaning of Christianity or to the requirements for salvation of which Christ spoke.

John Paul II is trying to strike a balance in re-asserting both the Church's Vatican II humanistic and supernatural priorities. He has few peers as a humanist, but he is also the Pope of the Catholic Church committed to a kingdom which basically is not intended to be of this world. A pope's voice is authoritative only as long as it seems to be Christ's voice, the voice of God's only begotten Son, born of the Virgin Mary, risen from the dead, the judge finally of the living and dead, founder of the Catholic Church whose function is to bring men through faith, sacraments and good life to their final resting place in the Communion of Saints, where they are to live everlastingly with their own resurrected bodies. These are the Christian basics now in doubt among the faithful by virtue of false teaching at every level of Catholic life. If the Pope has begun to enforce the policy of the Catholic Church (not his own), two questions come to mind. Where is the source of the contemporary Catholic problem? There are those who think the chief difficulty is not among theologians, but in the scripture scholars who tend to raise doubts whether we any longer can talk about the Word of God at all. The second question presumes God has spoken, but asks: Are the American bishops in their respective dioceses, through Catholic institutions and their own central agencies following the policies customarily associated with both bishops and popes?

Introduction

An American bishop, basking in the pleasant memories of the visit of John Paul II to the U.S., returned to Rome early in 1980 for a visit with the triumphant Pope. His audience, coming at the end of the Dutch Synod, afforded the bishop an opportunity to say to the Pope: "You know, your Holiness, we have at least six Hollands in the United States." To which the Pope replied in part: "I am most preoccupied with the Church in America."

It may surprise some that a bishop of the hitherto flourishing American Church would liken its present condition to Dutch Catholicism which after 1962 fell to a decrepit state in Catholic observance and, in the views of many observers, into a "de facto schism" from Rome. The prelate did not imply that American Catholic problems were of the same magnitude, but that there were similarities in the disarray of both churches. He also had in mind that forces were at work in the U.S. as in Holland to forestall any effort by John Paul II to stabilize the Catholic Church everywhere on Roman terms.

More than one bishop would agree that anti-Vatican forces do have considerable influence within American Catholicism. The problem, however, is deeper than anti-Romanism. What seems to be at stake is the meaning of Catholicism itself and who best represents its ancient revelation. Obvious efforts are being made to identify the Polish Pope with a narrow view both of faith and church. These attempts will not likely succeed (because John Paul II is saying nothing that Paul VI had not said many times before) but they do tend to keep the Church in turmoil. The difference now, however, is that the present Pope, unlike his predecessor and with support from the College of Cardinals, is moving to re-establish both orthodoxy and discipline. He made his first move to do this with the Dutch Synod.

But what about the American situation? Is John Paul II likely to make a difference for Catholics and for their bishops? Chicago sociologist Andrew Greeley seems to think he will make no difference at all, except perhaps to Catholic rightists who are "screaming for more blood" and to "the left" which "is growing more reckless and defiant" (*NY Daily News*, 8 June 1980). If Greeley is right the Church is in worse shape than most pastors realize. The Greeley Church would make the Pope's Chair as useful to Catholics as Queen Elizabeth's throne to the British people—a symbol, little more. Peter's Primacy would still be an honorable title, but the Vicar of Christ would be removed from the scene.

Bishops tend to ignore Greeley because they still see a large amount of piety wherever they go. Their parish visitations and diocesan rallies make them confident about the future of Catholicism. Surprisingly the Catholic "left" (unless the Pope cracks down hard) also looks upon this period of change in the Church as an exciting time to be Catholic. The literature, they say, even about polarization, is testimony to the Church's vitality, a *Deferred Revolution* in Walter Goddijn's terms, a *Second Spring* and the coming of age of U.S. Catholicism if Charles Fracchia is correct. Only conservative Catholics seem depressed, a mood capsulated by Louis Bouyer's *The Decomposition of Catholicism* (Chicago: Franciscan Herald Press, 1969).

The critical question, however, may not be the one asked by the pessimists: "Will Catholicism Survive?" but the one raised by post-conciliar optimists: "How do we de-Romanize the Church?" Edward Wakim and Joseph Scheuer wrote a book on that subject as early as 1966. Are there really six "Little Hollands" in the United States? Where do the American bishops stand vis-a-vis the Pope? If John Paul's doctrinal pronouncements and disciplinary decisions are normative for Roman institutions and bishops everywhere, will American bishops effectively bring their own dioceses into line? Or, while giving lip-service to John Paul, will they allow his leadership to erode at grassroot levels as Paul VI's was eroded?

Greeley's dour skepticism about Catholic compliance to papal directives may be set aside for the moment while attention is given to the basic religious question of our time: What did Christ really reveal that is important to modern man? The Dutch Church was in the process of providing its own answer, one which Rome does not like. "Six Little Hollands" in the United States pose an entirely new problem for Rome. The Vatican's relationship with the Dutch bishops is now part of the public record. Less attention has been paid to the fact that Rome has had the United States Church under scrutiny for some time. Vatican declarations on sexual and other ethical questions, on abuses in marriage triunals and liturgical celebrations, on first confession, on Catholic higher education were more often directed against the anti-Roman tendencies of important American Catholics than against Dutch dissidents. These Roman interventions would never have taken place had important Catholic institutions in the United States observed the Roman decrees implementing Vatican II. Instead, the violations became numerous, scrutiny by Rome was resented and—in the age of Watergate—the deviance was covered up by the American bishops. Vatican II was hardly old news when religious institutions here began to deny bishops the right to pass judgment on their performance, to say nothing of their Catholicity. Whereas the chief officers of an institution are normally held accountable for the success or failure of the enterprise, the bishops did little actual leading or supervising. Within this ecclesiastical climate the "little Hollands" developed, a story told often during the pontificate of Paul VI. Has the ascendancy of John Paul II made any difference?

Will an examination of six areas of Catholic life since the accession of John Paul II provide evidence of a difference? It is not possible to know which areas the Bishop mentioned above had in mind, but the following six centers of contemporary Catholic life are badly divided and in many aspects are out of step with the Church's teaching and practice (1) Catholic Universities and Colleges, (2) Catholic Theological Community, (3) Religious Communities, (4) Catholic Press, (5) the *United States Catholic Conference* (USCC), (6) Individual bishops themselves. Let us examine each of these in turn.

The Autonomous Catholic Universities and Their Theologians

1

The first arena where the continuing struggle with Rome is highly visible is the Catholic college campus. The theological community which handles most of classroom teaching is the second. It is no longer the struggle which is so important as the deleterious effects of the conflict on young Catholic lives, now accepted as a fact of life.

Consider *the Catholic institutions of higher learning* themselves. They may be more important to the integrity of American Catholicism than ever before. Factually, the Catholic college population is the only growing segment of Catholic education. Catholic colleges enroll twenty percent more students than they did in 1965, even though the number of these institutions has declined by about ten percent. (In the same period the student population of Catholic high schools declined by twenty percent, elementary schools by fifty percent.) If Catholic colleges are growing because they are supposedly Catholic, or for the Catholic advantages they are presumed to provide but do not, then the Church faces an institutional problem of the first magnitude.

A few examples will indicate that John Paul will have to exert a great deal more influence before one notices a change in what goes on today on Catholic campuses.

- Alfred Kazin, a New York Jewish professor, as visiting professor at Notre Dame during the 1978-1979 school year, finds himself "defending John Paul II to many Catholic religious and ex-religious" (*Notre Dame Magazine*, February, 1980).
- A student, James Attridge, writing for his peers at the University of San Francisco (*Foghorn*, 21 March 1980) finds "a lot of things about Catholicism in 1980 stink." He tells why: (1) "If you are going to have a

religious requirement in a university or secondary school, it would be a good idea to include something about Catholicism; (2) "Today's Church devotes inadequate energy to clarifying to its own exactly what it is about"; (3) "People my age of the Catholic persuasion grew up in the Vatican II mishmash in which no one knew what to think."

- Mt. St. Vincent's College, the foundation of New York's Sisters of Charity, justifies an honorary degree for a pro-abortion Congressman on the grounds that it is "no longer a Catholic college", even though its main appeal for funds and students is to the local Catholic community.
- *NC News* announced May 27, 1981 that Fr. Joseph A. Komonchak, a New York priest, will be scholar-in-residence at the North American College in Rome (the U.S. bishops' seminary) for the academic year 1981-1982. His role there (according to *NC*) will be to participate in "the academic and pastoral formation" of the future leaders of the American Church. From the time of his ordination in 1964 Fr. Komonchak was one of the earliest defenders of the right of public dissent from Church doctrine on contraception. Scarcely five years after his ordination he joined Charles Curran in 1969 in producing the volume *Contraception: Authority and Dissent*. Almost ten years later Komonchak was still at work seeking to "communicate an understanding, if not an acceptance, of the widespread dissent *Humanae Vitae* has occasioned" (*Theological Studies*, June 1978, p. 257). At least three bishops had to pass on this appointment. The question rightly comes to mind: Did any one of them think Fr. Komonchak's negative influence on American seminarians' priestly formation a matter of importance?

These strange results of Catholic education are commonplace on many other campuses and are the direct outgrowth of regular dissent in today's Catholic college classroom. At a leading Catholic university, for example, an ex-religious opens his course on the sacrament of matrimony by distributing a mimeograph sheet asking his young learners to contemplate the following question in advance: "Is the moral teaching of the magisterium binding on the Catholic conscience?" His answer: "Dissent is possible." Learning dissent before the doctrines to which they normally should assent as Catholics is not the customary pedagogical approach one expects. The students at the Catholic University of America receive dissent as a steady diet. The student newspaper there gained notoriety during 1980 as result of advertising a homosexual meeting on campus. Two priest faculty members rushed in with the public advice that homosexual acts are not necessarily sinful in all instances. One even said it could be "a morally good thing to do" (*National Catholic Register*, 27 April 1980).

Occurrences of these kinds are not occasional incidents but presently pervade Catholic higher education. Dissent is more deeply imbedded in its infrastructures today than in 1967 when Charles Curran humbled the American bishops by his strike at Catholic University of America. And the reason is quite simple: Catholic higher education has detached itself from the authority of the Church and a fortiori from the binding force of Church teaching. The *Association of Catholic Colleges and Universities* (ACCU), for example, has recently abandoned any attempt to formalize Catholic college identity (*Update*, June 1980, p. 3). ACCU took this position in spite of a warning from Fr. James Burtchaell that the need to hide Catholic identity (due to pressure, he said, from Jesuit universities and New York colleges, 20 or 23 colleges had secularized to be eligible for state aid) will lead to their secularization or demise. The ACCU rejected Burtchaell's advice and endorsed instead the position of the *Catholic Theological Society of America* (CTSA).

Three months after the 1980 Bishops meeting (February 3-4, 1981) the ACCU held its annual meeting in Washington, D.C. with Fr. Richard McBrien invited as keynote speaker "to situate the Catholic college and university in the context of the total mission of the Church for today and the decade." Executive director Sr. Alice Gallin chose him because she thought he might help ACCU implement the Bishops' recent pastoral on Catholic higher education. The Notre Dame theologian seized the opportunity to instruct the 250 conference attendants how their institutions might profit from the "ecclesiological advances taken by the Second Vatican Council."

McBrien's recommended approach was based on the proposition that "it is ecclesiastically archaic to use the noun church to mean only the Catholic Church." And since Catholicism no longer has the necessary mission "to bring everybody in" or to emphasize its institutional nature, theologians must ask themselves: Do they serve the hierarchy or "the entire community of the baptized"? In their turn Catholic college educators must also recognize that yielding Catholicism "too quickly to ecclesiastical pressure sins not only against good ecclesiology but against the intellectual integrity and the maturity of faith of its own people." McBrien's conviction that the Church is more *People* than *Hierarchy* led him to suggest to his audience the possibility that "a college or university might begin to see itself as an entirely independent enterprise within the Church" and one "holding itself theologically accountable to no Catholic agency outside the school."

ACCU, which has been the regular point of contact on higher education matters between Rome and the American hierarchy, hardly needed McBrien's theological motivation to demand further autonomy from the Church. Sr. Alice Gallin and Msgr. Frederick McManus, chairman of ACCU's Board, went to Rome seeking exemption for United States colleges from any overview by American bishops and/or the Holy See. The proposed new Code of Canon Law, for example, intends to assert the hierarchy's rights over Catholic colleges and the colleges' obligation to the Church. Gallin and McManus, using McBrien's arguments by intuition in 1978, sought to frustrate Rome's effort to re-establish a juridical relationship between the hierarchy of the Church and Catholic higher education in the United States. If that effort failed, ACCU intended to involve the hierarchy in anti-establishment legalisms to such an extent as to make canon law on Catholic college behavior meaningless. Their report on the new Code's revisions, while conceding the rights of ecclesiastical authority "at some point," objects to a "canonical mission" for theologians in a Catholic college (as if theologicans speak on their own authority) because they see that mission already implicit in their baptism. McManus looks upon this mission (for the most part for priests and/or religious) as "perilous to the academic integrity and the civil and academic recognition of our institutions." Alice Gallin warns further that Rome's action may force Catholic colleges to give up "the name and identity of Catholic." This is a threat used against bishops and Rome since 1970 and was carried out whenever it suited Catholic college convenience, as in New York State from 1968 onward. Msgr. McManus makes the point that the proposed canons on higher education for 1981 onward are not found in the 1917 Code. He does not indicate that in 1917 (and up until 1967) there was no need for Church legislation of this kind for the good reason that Catholic colleges, by voluntary act of their sponsoring religious communities and faculty, subjected themselves to Catholic law and Catholic standards of theological teaching. The proposed new canons have historical significance. They recognize the fact that today large numbers of Catholic colleges wish to trade on the Church's tradition in higher education without necessarily confessing responsibility to the Catholic hierarchy who are the only unitary guardians the Catholic Church possesses. As premier theologian Henri de Lubac states the case: "The Church we call our Mother is not some ideal and unreal Church but this hierarchical Church herself...The obedience which we pledge her in the persons of those who rule cannot be anything but filial obedience." (See his *Splendour of the Church*, esp. pp. 196-197.)

Fr. McBrien presented the ACCU conference with what he saw as a realistic picture for our times:

> A Catholic institution of higher learning which happens to be situated in a diocese whose bishop is theologically very much to the right will feel compelled to meet one standard of orthodoxy and Church discipline. A Catholic institution of higher learning in a diocese whose bishop is more theologically advanced and more sensitive to the inevitable pluralism of

contemporary theology will find itself with a much greater measure of latitude and freedom in constructing its curricula and programs.

On February 28, 1981 *ACCU Update* (p. 1) summarized for its membership the significance of the McBrien keynote address: "The need for a deep understanding of the ecclesiology of Vatican II was stressed as a prelude of reflection on the University's own self-understanding."

In its turn a committee of the Catholic Theological Society of America looks upon John Paul II's effort to regulate pontifical and ecclesiastical faculties (*Sapientia Christiana*) not only as "alarming" but as "ominous." The theological group maintains that the papal constitution "cannot be implemented in the North American context without serious harm." Why so? Because *Sapientia Christiana* (and the proposed new Code of Canon Law) insist that the Catholic teachers teach not on their own authority but "by virtue of the mission they have received from the Church", i.e., as the result of a canonical mission. CTSA views canonically erected or approved schools as possibly paying "a very high price for the privilege of granting pontifical degrees."

The Catholic University's Presidential Advisory Committee also opposes important requirements of *Sapientia Christiana*: the requirements for canonical mission, ecclesiastical degrees and the Roman *nihil obstat* for professors. Since CUA is the most prominent institution to be affected by Roman legislation, the President's committee also thinks the Pope's insistence on the professor's "upright life" or "moral life" requires special study for its application in the context of American law, although an upright and moral life is normally expected of professors in Catholic institutions, regardless of the civil law context.

These successive rejections of a juridical place in the Church by bodies of Catholic academics are themselves ominous. The college leaders involved in these rejections call for more dialogue with bishops as a substitute for confrontation. ACCU's Msgr. John Murphy once assured Cardinal Cooke (March 2, 1976) that the Higher Education Committee of the *United States Catholic Conference (USCC)*, chaired by Archbishop Borders, was received with the warmest approval in the collegiate world. However, dialogue seems never to bring concessions from the academicians, while it does prevent the hierarchy from taking its own steps to protect the faith of the Church.

Ominous, too, is the unknown extent of dissent in the major seminaries of the country. That it exists is unquestionable. Charles Curran keeps a strict control over the moral theology taught to seminarians at Catholic University. Anthony Kosnick, the chief author of the book *Human Sexuality* (New York: Paulist Press, 1977), censured by the American bishops and the Holy See, teaches in a seminary. There are reports extant of courses given in which seminarians are regularly fed dissent even about the sexual practices in their own supposedly celibate lives, of ex-priest dissenters invited to give them lectures, of 'gay' activism (duly reported at times in 'gay' literature), of professors denying the historicity of the miracle stories of the New Testament, even instilling doubts about the Virgin Birth. Bishops have withdrawn their candidates from such places because of unhappiness with the effects of this training, only to complain of the difficulty they have in finding sound alternates.

The *National Catholic Reporter* (6 February 1981) gave an account of a human sexuality program conducted at St. John's Seminary in Clement, Michigan, which fell under the jurisdiction of the Archbishop of Detroit. *NCR* reported the workshops as planned to motivate future priests to be "in touch with their own sexuality" so that they can properly advise couples on marital and sexual matters. What *NCR* did not report was that six films were shown to seminarians which were pornographic in the explicit depiction of male and female masturbation, overt homosexual and lesbian displays, and adultery between an older couple. One private reviewer considered that "the films are designed, photographed and presented in seminars in order to seduce people into primarily intellectual acceptance of immorality."

If seventy-one per cent of the American priesthood now disagrees with *Humanae Vitae,* it is not surprising to hear that seventy-two percent of Catholic married couples do not live by its norms. The issue here is not simply contraception but the theological perspective which has been provided seminarians and young priests since 1965. Seminaries, usually under the direct control of bishops, are responsible for the orthodoxy of priests, on whom the future well-being of the Church depends.

It is for this reason that the *Fellowship of Catholic Scholars* considers that John Paul's *Sapientia Christiana* meets a "crucial need" for both college students and seminarians. The Fellowship sees the real issue in Catholic higher education to be the following:

> In the past decade and a half, many of the teachings of the Church authoritatively proclaimed by the magisterium in the exercise of its mission to bring the full truth of the gospel to all mankind and to protect the Body of doctrine committed to its trust have met serious opposition within the Church. This has been true not merely of peripheral questions or new problems but of substantive issues of faith and morals that have been received as Catholic teaching for centuries and that have been strongly reaffirmed in recent years after careful deliberation. At times certain teachings of the Church have been rejected by scholars as erroneous or historically and culturally conditioned. Among those opposing and even rejecting the authoritative and authentic teaching of the Church are theologians, some

of whom were engaged in teaching seminarians. Newly ordained priests and seminarians are at time of the opinion that their special mission within the Church is to liberate the faithful from what they consider to be the intolerable and unnecessary burdens imposed on them by the magisterium. In their turn hitherto faithful Christians have been led to believe it is now right and proper to depart from the authoritative teaching of the Church on many questions (*Newsletter* September 1980, p. 9).

At the center of the Catholic university problem are *rebellious theologians*.

Older theologians did not recognize any broad right to dissent from teachings proposed in a non-infallible mode by the authentic magisterium. Scholars spoke then of the possibility of withholding assent to teachings while such questions were studied. Eventually they submitted dubious hypotheses to this hierarchy. John A. Ryan and John Courtney Murray, SJ, took this for granted, as readily as Francis Connell, CSSR, and John C. Ford, SJ. When the move to accommodate American mores began to dominate the thinking of educators like Fr. Theodore Hesburgh and Fr. Robert Henle, and theologians like Fr. Charles Curran, Catholic higher education began to change. A new approach toward hierarchy became visible and an anti-magisterium tone began to spread from college to college. Theologians made it clear that discipline by authority figures was no longer acceptable. Social control only from peers was to be the rule, they said.

The Fellowship of Catholic Scholars, on the other hand, estimates the Catholic problem to be not so much freedom of scholars as the truth of revelation. An obscure French theologian named Jacques Pohier received a certain notoriety (and a defense from scholars) because Rome penalized him for his theological views. Few Americans know that Dominican Pohier's book *When I Say God* rendered doubtful the following elements of Christian revelation: the sacrificial value of Christ's death, his corporeal resurrection, eternal life, God's transcendence, the real presence of Christ in the Eucharist, the role of the priest in the Eucharist, the divinity of Christ and the exercise of infallibility in the Church. A Church which did not face up to such a challenge to its fundamental teaching would jeopardize its following. Yet, as far as academics were concerned, Pohier's rights and the Vatican's procedures for judging him were matters of a higher order than his doubts about the Catholic faith.

The French Dominican may only be more incautious about his disbelief than important Americans. But disbelief of one kind or another is not a rare expression among scholars in the United States. Fr. John McKenzie wrote *The Old Testament Without Illusions* (Chicago: Thomas More Press, 1979), in which he leaves open the basic question of "what it means to call the Bible the Word of God" (p. 263). The best that a reviewer for *Theological Studies* could say in response to this *dubium* (June 1980, p. 438) is that "[McKenzie] closes with the suggestion that the Bible is probably better understood as a record of human response to God's presence and activity, a response in which 'God is revealed sometimes better, sometimes not so well.' " This sentiment hardly makes the Bible any more important than the Koran, an idea underscored by Brother Gabriel Moran when he indicted the Catholic bishops for their failure to recognize (in approving the *National Catholic Directory*) that "public revelation of God" is also contained in Hinduism (*National Catholic Reporter*, 19 January 1979, p. 16).

The Catholic issue must not be seen, therefore, as this or that opinion of a single or a few theologians, nor the general anti-Roman attitude of their frequently quoted representatives. The Church suffers only mildly when a Fr. Walter Burghardt, editor of *Theological Studies*, while defending Hans Kung, tells the secular press: "Do not question my faith or fidelity if I choke on the Doctrinal Congregations' arguments condemning all direct sterilization." (*N.Y. Times*, 8 April 1980); or when Richard McBrien, the new chairman of the theology department at Notre Dame, tells the Catholic Press in the same month: "What John Paul says to the Dutch won't change what's happening in a good American parish" (*Brooklyn Tablet*, 29 April 1980).

On the other hand, critical to the peaceful functioning of the Church is the denial by the body of theologians that bishops and pope run the Church. CTSA, speaking of cooperation with bishops, reveals in one of its unpublished reports assumptions under which American theologians operate and which underlie much of their *praxis*:

1. There are different concepts of revelation, church and church authority at work in the Church, not confined to those enunciated by the magisterium.
2. Theologians will determine who and what a Catholic theologian is—not the canonical mission from bishops or pope.
3. Theologians will determine when the magisterium serves the word of God.
4. Theologians have the right and duty to question Church statements.
5. If theologians must be judged by an outsider, it is preferable that this be done by the local bishop (rather than Rome), as long as the local bishop listens to diverse views.

A published report of ongoing discussions of certain theologians with American bishops further proposes that the bishop is better called a spokesman for the faith than a teacher, limits bishops' authority to teach, legitimizes dissent, and expresses preference for occasional joint statements by bishops and theologians to statements by bishops alone (*Origins,* 7 February 1980, pp. 541 ff). Among the document's most pungent sentences are the following:

> "It is usually prudent for bishops to avoid taking a position when theologians have not reached a consensus" (p. 544).
> "[There are] no sources reserved to the bishops alone over and above the sources of revelation" (p. 546).
> "Can truth be taught by authority? Can we accept as part of our faith the idea that one can reach truth through an authority established for this purpose in the Church?" (p. 549).
> "The local bishop does not just echo or extend Rome's teaching, but in some way influences it" (p. 549).

These sentiments reflect the CTSA's desire to limit the bishop's role in the Church and to divide bishops from Rome, while denying to Church authority the right to "silence" those who teach contrary to the magisterium. *The Joint Committee of Catholic Learned Societies* (December 6, 1977) reinforces the same trend when it expresses anxiety that dioceses (e.g. Washington) are now scrutinizing catechetical materials and the doctrinal programs for seminarians (as if this does not truly represent the competence of bishops). Avery Dulles even sees a threat to scholars in the Vatican censure of Jesuit John McNeill's promotion of homosexuality (as if public toleration of such deviance would not be a threat to Catholic moral values).

What, then, is the Church's central problem with theologians? It is simply this: The popular form of theologizing today, even within Catholicism, is non-denominational, i.e. speculating about sacred things hardly constrained at all by Church definitions, bearing little of the stamp of the religious community which ostensibly the theologians are supposed to serve. The new name for this theology is *revisionism*, illustrated for Catholics by Fr. David Tracy's *Blessed Rage for Order* (New York: Seabury Press, 1975). This book claims that even an updated orthodoxy (neo-orthodoxy) is no longer viable for the Catholicism we can expect to see develop out of Vatican II.

Revisionist theology is a secular (not a sacred) science. It begins not with revelation but with man's faith experience, with our "basic faith" in the transcendant. One-time Catholic University of America professor Fr. William Shea after reading Tracy concluded that "the Catholic hierarchic principle in its application to theology is shredded" (*Anglican Theological Review* 1976 vol. 58, no. 3, p. 265). Revisionism shreds more than the Church's hierarchy. It puts an end to man's hierarchical relationship with God himself. A theology which concentrates on man's religious experience is not theology (i.e. the study of God) but religious anthropology or the sociology of religion. Revelation as an objective reality is excluded from this study. If God as transcendent being is considered at all it is solely from a human perspective and as part of a scholar's search to explain man's mysterious and universal need to reach beyond himself for his complete meaning. Shea describes how the secular theologian approaches his study:

> The theologian is to approach all beliefs critically. Secularity implies that all traditions, authorities, doctrines, dogmas, and beliefs are questionable and indeed, must be questioned. The fact that something is believed is in no way evidence for its truth. Nor can any authority be allowed to vouch for the truth of beliefs whether that authority be the Bible, credal expressions, or an office in the Church. The loyalty of the theologian to Church or traditions does not involve taking beliefs to be true; it only means that they will be taken seriously and put under scrutiny. The theologian furthermore, will accept traditional Christian self-understanding only insofar as it does not negate fundamental secular faith. The true understanding of Christianity will be in harmony with basic faith, for Christian faith *can* be none other than the most adequate articulation of the basic faith of secularity. Traditional beliefs will be interpreted in harmony with that basic faith and negated when they conflict with it (*ibid.*, p. 267).

It is important to realize the significance of this judgment. Qualified scholars determine what Christianity means, not evangelists, not priests, not even popes.

This is not what the Second Vatican Council said:

> "Sacred tradition and sacred scripture make up a single sacred deposit of the Word of God, which is entrusted to the Church... the task of giving an authentic interpretation of the Word of God whether in its written form or in the form of tradition has been entrusted to the living teaching authority of the Church alone. Its authority in this matter is exercised in the name of Jesus Christ." (*Dogmatic Constitution on Divine Revelation* No. 10.)

Obviously this differs radically from the way revisionist theologians approach Church pronouncements. William Shea, for example, capsulates the revisionist's principles as follows: (1) a "truth" of faith is not to be accepted on its face value as true; (2) loyalty to the Church or to the faith of the people is not his primary concern; (3) the revisionist theologian need not be a believer at all; (4) theology is a science independent of the Church; (5) theology is a secular, not a sacred, science; (6) theological enquiry is autonomous to the exclusion of non-scientific authorities; (7) pragmatism is the philosophical base of the revisionist method; (8) human experience is the norm for determining the truth of theological knowledge.

Not all dissenting theologians are as blunt as Shea about their detachment from the Church or the Bible, but very many today insist on "autonomy" from Church authority and freedom to decide for themselves against the hierarchy, if need be, what constitutes the essentials of the Catholic faith. The quest for autonomy which underpinned the 1967 Land O'Lakes declaration of independence by 26 Catholic educators explains the resistance in 1981 to John Paul's *Sapientia Christiana* within the Catholic University of America's School of Religious Studies. So powerful is the passion for autonomy that even some contemporary theologians seeking to maintain their own orthodoxy feel it more important to accommodate themselves to revisionism more than to be known as outspoken defenders of the magisterium. That this kind of accommodation is so common is precisely what gives dissenters respectability in the groves of secular academe, regardless of Rome's disfavor or the effect of doctrinal deviance on the faith of the Catholic people. An indication of the ease with which American theologians tip toward revisionism was the presentation of the 1980 *John Courtney Murray Award* by CTSA to revisionist David Tracy.

Within this context we must judge what has happened to Catholic college and university life in the United States. These institutions, as we said earlier, are not abstractions or disembodied organs of learning. They are corporations which, whatever the legal requirements for civil status, owe their origins to a religious body subject to Church law. They are corporations which, whatever the composition of their present Boards of Trustees, specify themselves as Catholic and claim that identity in their appeal for faculty, students and funds. They are corporations which, whatever their secular purpose, justify their independent existence and demand for Catholic support by the services they perform in the name of Catholicism. A Catholic college may profess secular allegiance to the state or country in which it is chartered, British, German, Japanese, or American (and a willingness to observe reasonable regulation by governmental bodies and nationally distinct professional associations) but its *finis operis*, its ultimate objective, its reason for being is to work for the advantage of the Catholic faith. This involves, one would expect, a minimum of institutional commitment to the propositions of faith of the Church and to the Catholic hierarchy which is the final judge of what those propositions mean. Even at the level of abstract research in doctrinal matters (actually a small percentage of Catholic academic operations) this commitment is a sacred one for scholars who work or who would work within the context of their Catholic faith.

The present sore point of Catholic tension can be found here. Catholic scholars and Catholic institutions now want to work outside the Catholic context, without a commitment to hierarchical overview, and still call themselves Catholic. Since 1967 they have staked out a position of independence from the hierarchy of the Catholic Church. By offering themselves as rivals and alternate teachers of contradictory religious doctrines in the mould of secular university professors they make conflict with the hierarchy and the subornation of the Catholic faith inevitable.

Some scholars try to make this palatable in a variety of ways. They merely avoid taking public positions on certain doctrinal questions whenever they are in opposition to Catholic teaching. But their audiences know where they stand on those subjects. Others pretend to be even-handed. They present the pope's position on one page, the opinions of contemporary theologians on the other, leaving choices with the reader. Readers, however, have a good idea where these teachers really stand. Then there are scholarly types who while professing fidelity to Church formulas raise interminable questions to which they never provide answers, to which they never feel the need to provide answers. As scientists they are engaged in an inevitable search for elusive truth, which they, not the magisterium, may one day discover, but not yet. Listeners smile at scholars' ingenuity in eluding the officers of the magisterium. Yet the scholars hope to persuade Church officers that their implied or suggested doctrinal reformulations are legitimate compromises with modernity and are authentically Catholic even after the Holy See has denied this repeatedly.

The dissenting scholars easier to deal with may be (they may not be) those who admit their dissent but say it is only '5 percent'. They allege, as if it were the virtue of Catholic faith being exercised, that they are in ninety-five percent agreement with pope and bishops on Catholic doctrine. Yet, when one examines the five percent they doubt or reject, it is clear that more often than not certain core Catholic doctrines are being questioned or rejected. Furthermore, a scholar's five percent heresy or deviance, if legitimated, automatically confers on every other Catholic the right in good conscience to choose his own five percent area of denial. In these circumstances there will not be lacking those who feel justified in raising their personal ante for continued membership in the Church to ten percent heresy or deviance. Such "pick and choose" Catholicism makes the Church *in principle* a congregation of believers, half-believers, and hangers-on (which *in fact* she has often been) and denies her divinely established role as the *House of God* and the *Body of Christ* in possession of the Keys to man's eternal salvation. (In making this assertion we acknowledge the complexity of theological issues at the scholars' and confessors' level, the difference between divine faith statements or Catholic doctrine defined by the ordinary or extraordinary magisterium from the common teachings of Catholic theologians but not formally taught as the doctrine of the Church. These legitimate distinctions, intended to aid scholars and confessors in making moral judgments, were never designed to reduce faith in Christ and his Church to a quantitative minimum.)

Presently, however, theological and doctrinal doubts among the faithful reach into substantive areas of Catholic faith. They may not always be expressed as formal denials but uncertainty about revelation and what it means when unattended leads inevitably to formal denial or quiet heresy/schism. When scholars say that they have the right to dissent they assert the faithfuls' right to determine for themselves what the faith is, what is required for them to receive the sacraments, and for salvation, what is and is not sin, and so forth. If sustained, the right of dissent does give the faithful the corresponding right of free choice in religious matters. Whatever form of religion this might be, it is not Catholicism. One-time Jesuit novice Charles A. Fracchia describing the "Second Spring" of U.S. Catholicism (in a new book with this name [New York: Harper & Row, 1980]) describes a new spirituality as follows: "Many people today believe personal union with God to be equally, if not more important than intellectual acceptance of religious precepts" (p. 166). Whatever spirituality this may be, it is not even Christian.

It would be a mistake to think that only academic persons offend against Catholic doctrine by denying it or explaining it away. Pastors or curates, the Church's first ministers of the Word and the last guarantors of that word for Catholic parishioners, are found in many places encouraging defiance of Church definitions and expected practice. One new Rhode Island pastor came home from theological updating in Kansas with the conviction that Catholics should disavow the notion that their church has one unbending universal teaching on all moral issues. He told the religious educators of Providence that there is "much exercise of teaching authority in the Church that is dogmatic." When confronted by a married woman in the audience with *Humanae Vitae*, the Rhode Island pastor countered with the assertion that the "confusion in the Church would have been less if Pope Paul had admitted that he made a mistake and that the encyclical reflected his own opinion" (*The Providence Sunday Journal*, 21 March 1981).

The Fellowship of Catholic Scholars published what is called a "realistic description of what goes on in many theological faculties". The FCS report spoke of the doubts presently being engendered among the faithful about "the divinity of Christ, the origins and infallibility of the Church, the importance of sacraments to Christian life, the relevance of the priesthood and religious life itself." The result, FCS scholars conclude, is that many Catholics "believe it now is right and proper to depart from the authoritative teaching of the Church on many questions." The FCS, merely highlight a problem with which Rome has been grappling since 1967.

There can be no peace with Rome or on Catholic university campuses as long as these conditions continue to exist.

Religious Superiors and Religious Editors Follow Suit

2

If a "Little Holland" is defined as a segment of the Church resisting or fighting Rome, then two additional Catholic institutions in the United States give evidence of schismatic tendencies—religious communities and the secondary life-line of Catholic communication (after educational institutions), otherwise known as the Catholic press. Some would insist that the breakdown of religious community solidarity with Church authority preceded rather than followed other forms of Catholic malaise, that Catholic press leaders (like Robert Hoyt in the *National Catholic Reporter*, John Cogley of *Commonweal* and Fr. John Reedy of Ave Maria Press) were fashioners of popular dissent at least contemporaneous with secular-minded theologians and university presidents. Be that as it may, few would argue that neither institutional religious life nor the Catholic press can anymore be counted on as a certainty to reinforce the institutional belief and value system of the Catholic Church.

Secularized and disobedient religious are sometimes placed in the front ranks of those who have misused the spirit and documents of Vatican II. Louis Bouyer's little book *Priests and Religious Against God* is an account of how the Church's religious—select members of Catholic communities committed by vow to gospel, poverty, chastity, and obedience—are now a powerful Catholic voice for worldliness and at times for enmity to the sacred. If dissident academicians sparked intellectual doubt among the Church's faithful, rebellious religious men and women have become a source of unusual scandal to other religious and to the faithful. This was hardly the result contemplated by the Council Fathers' call for renewal of the spirit, forms and apostolates of religious life. They had no idea that the end result of "renewal" would be revolution within prestigious religious communities. No one in Council affairs foresaw monks and nuns leading charges against important institutions of the Church itself. The Jesuit and Maryknoll communities, the School Sisters of St. Francis and the Sisters of Mercy are by now well known examples of how successful apostolates are abandoned or distorted to work against the purposes for which they received Church authorization in the first place.

Doubly harmful effects fell upon the Church body because these same rebellious religious communities affected badly the work of the many Catholic colleges and important Church ministries they controlled. Catholic higher education was secularized almost overnight because religious superiors used their absolute power over subjects to this end. Diocesan clergy, who lived the equivalent of a laissez-faire existence under bishops, rarely felt the same pressure. An anti-Roman bishop did not have the power (at least in the short run) to turn his priests against the pope. On the other hand, religious superiors controlling a tight machinery whenever they chose to determine its course, including their subjects' "vow of obedience", possessed unusual power. On their own initiative or as a result of pressure from rebels in the ranks they began to enforce new rules on those who stood for traditional values or for the pope. The "silencing" in 1980 of Fr. Cornelius M. Buckley, SJ, for criticizing Jesuit dissenters on the West Coast is only a recent example of the disciplinary direction since 1965 of many religious communities. Similar pressures are almost unknown in the world of the diocesan clergy or in any situation where the ecclesial authority is a bishop.

The defiance of Church law continues unabated. Sr. Diane Drufenbrock ran for Vice-President of the United States on a Socialist ticket in 1980, while Fr. James Noonan, Superior General of Maryknoll, called upon priests in the same year to remain in politics despite the Vatican's prohibition. (*New York Daily News*, 10 August 1980). One lightly reported story of that year was the resignation of Sr. Joan Gormley as the major office of the Maryland Province of the Sisters of Notre Dame de Namur because she no longer thought her community deserved the name Catholic. Writing to members of her community in private correspondence (February 18, 1980) she said:

> At stake in our disregard for the Voice of the Church is our life within the Church. This is no small thing. I believe all of us will be required to choose how we want to live our religious life. For myself finding a contradiction between the congregation and the Church, I choose to listen to the Church.

The story of the alienation of important religious communities parallels that of Catholic colleges and a detailed account of this story is redundant in view of the full accounts detailed in many sources.

Less well documented in the public forum is the process of harassment and intimidation going on within religious life in accordance with canon law and Vatican directives—or who insist on teaching orthodox doctrine. "New" religious presidents and their councils penalize those who refuse to abandon their commitment to their vows or obedience to the teaching authority of the Church. Traditional religious within communities and traditional communities themselves, though encouraged by Rome, frequently lack support from local bishops. They complain, too, that appointments to diocesan posts often go to religious who lead a secular life and who wear secular clothes. Not infrequently "modern" community leaders contest the right of bishops to make demands upon them and are not above intimidating bishops ("we will remove our teachers") to get their way. In the meantime bishops themselves "to keep the peace" (as they say) are not above dismissing or allowing to be dismissed from teaching offices in their diocese, sisters, brothers or priests who in normal times would be considered the backbone of the Church's educational apostolate. Such passivity in episcopal chanceries not only demoralizes the "loyal" sons and daughters of the Church but cements the power of dissenting religious leadership.

Franciscan sister Yvonne Rowley sums up how the "modern" religious leadership got that way:

> Modernism had been subtly but successfully engrained in the minds of many unsuspecting sisters. They considered themselves the bearers of the current gospel and looked with pity upon their less enlightened companions. Error, under the guise of intellectualism, was freely shared through group dynamics, sensitivity training and other effective but destructive tactics. The sisters were gullible victims. Accustomed to trust those in authority (because, in most cases, they had earned that trust), the sisters absorbed the new ideas and began to propagate them to students and fellow Christians among the laity. (*Catholic Currents,* 15 April 1981, p. 4).

Probably the most important symbol of Catholic disintegration has been the breakdown of the Society of Jesus. Once the most formidable force for Catholic intellectualism and the single most pervasive influence in Catholic higher education (with twenty-seven colleges and universities), to say little of their profound influence on Catholic spirituality through retreat houses and mission centers, Ignatius Loyola's order became such a house divided against itself that a nationally known Jesuit once recommended that the Society be split into two groups if only to save legitimate religious life from complete erosion. Following the Council two of their famous theologates, Woodstock and Chicago, closed doors, and their respected publications *Theological Studies* and *America,* long known as standard-bearers of authentic Catholic intellectuality, became anti-Roman in tone and in content.

The Society at first reflected the negative stirrings going on in the larger Church, but in due course became itself a disintegrating force by virtue of the extensive network of Catholic institutions under the influence of its large membership. The failure of Jesuit leaders, like that of Roman officials and bishops, to "manage" the changes they were initiating or tolerating was surprising, considering their reputation prior to Vatican II for effectiveness. Internal conflict and lowered morale are natural by-products of change but a more provident management would have guided the transition more felicitously and guarded the Church's institutional values more surely. Instead, they facilitated widespread breakdown. Jesuit superiors permitted anti-institutional thinkers to dominate theologates, formation centers for novices and retreat houses, even before these spokesmen achieved status on university faculties. They dissipated almost overnight any semblance of group unity (and pride) by abandoning rules and by breaking up Jesuit houses into small group living establishments, where individual tastes and sometimes scandalous behavior reigned to the disillusionment of those attempting to maintain important Jesuit traditions.

The outward signs of disarray were not long in coming—decline in the number of novices and scholastics by as much as two-thirds, the loss of more than 600 priests in the United States alone (almost 2,000 world-wide), open defiance of Church regulations, even on the worship of the Eucharist, in-house "celebrations" when Jesuits departed the Order, subjects telling superiors what they would or would not do, cruel treatment of "traditionalists", denial of important Catholic doctrines in Jesuit conferences and classrooms, deviant behavior and bad example even by provincials and novice masters.

In 1941 Fr. John Courtney Murray conducted an ordination retreat for New York priests in which he stressed the importance of the virtue of fidelity, holding up his Jesuit community as a paradigm. Twenty-six years later and a few weeks before he died, Murray was bemoaning privately in the same city that fidelity was now in short supply among Jesuits. Fr. Joseph Becker, SJ, traces correctly causes of defections among Jesuits after 1958: the popular rise within the Church of four characteristics of modernity—stress on subjective satisfaction (rather than the objective service), acceptance of relativity as a rule of life (rather than absolute norms), priority of the individual over the group and the shift toward the value of this world (the secular) instead of idealizing the sacred in man and God, which historically shaped the forms of Catholic religious life (*Studies*, January-March 1977, pp. 70-71). These factors together clearly played their part in loosening the ties that bound religious to their communities. Yet, if one single factor looms as the *unifying* force in promoting disunity it was the process of "secularization", i.e. the loss of the sense and importance of "The Holy", the loss at times of supernatural faith itself. Becker cites the answer of a nun asked to comment on the loss in a five year period of 27,000 women from religious orders. Sr. Lois McGovern, OP, described it as "one of the most exciting things that has ever happened to the Church" (p. 32). Such hostility from a religious about her order's commitment explains in large part why communities suddenly collapsed, when they did not become negative forces within the ecclesial body. But it must be said by way of explanation that hostility of this kind did not arise by spontaneous generation; it was inculcated in Mother-houses throughout the Council years and immediately thereafter. With little opposition, too, from superiors and with some assistance from segments of the Catholic press and priests who used the secular press to denigrate the Church or its teaching. Louis Bouyer is certainly correct that "religious"—priests and nuns—have done the most damage to Catholic authenticity beginning with the Council (Redemptorist Bernard Haring is a good example) until the present day. The newest example of self-righteous Catholic masochism came from the pen of Redemptorist Francis X. Murphy who recently in the *Atlantic Monthly* (February 1981) caricatured Catholic teaching on Christian marriage, belittled the nature of the Church and compromised the existence of any divine revelation worth arguing about. Having failed during Vatican II to see his distorted views of Catholicism vindicated, Murphy here writes against the Church for an audience with more than its due share of native anti-Catholics. A member of a religious community known historically for preaching strict observance of Catholic norms, he distorts the Council record, vilifies the present pope, calls two Cardinals liars, and misuses the name of St. Alphonsus Ligouri, in about the same way his mentor Fr. Bernard Haring did during the meetings of the Pontifical Birth Control Commission in 1965-1966.

The strange aspect of this disedifying behavior by a religious priest is that Murphy, already on his way to oblivion, was recalled to prominence by his superiors and, in spite of a long record of deviance, ensconced as rector of Holy Redeemer College in Washington, D.C. where he presides over Redemptorist seminarians and young priests attending nearby Catholic University at the very time a new pope was chosen to restore a sense of discipline to the religious life of the

Church.

The misuse of the secular press, however, by dissident religious or apostate Catholics is only one side of the Church's communication problem. Far greater harm derives from a *secularized Catholic press*. Here we are dealing with the fourth "Little Holland", mention of which was made earlier.

Dutch Jesuit J. Bots alleges that in Holland the Catholic media actually were "the bearers" of the ideology which ultimately brought the Dutch Bishops to account before John Paul II. Dutch Jesuit William Peters also maintains that the reason Holland's Catholicism ran away from its tradition (and from Rome) was the bishops' fear of the repressive power of the press, often their own. The Church of Amsterdam, of Rotterdam, of Utrecht fell on evil days because bishops grew to be afraid of any action which gained them a bad public image. Dutch dissenters took tight control of Catholic communications away from Bishops and proceeded to fashion Holland's Catholics according to their new and anti-Roman ideology.

The media situation in the United States is somewhat different because no such centralized control of the Catholic press exists at the Church or state level. Nonetheless similarities to Holland do exist. As in Holland, the secular media are disposed to treat men like Hans Kung or Charles Curran favorably because they challenge the hierarchy or contest official Catholic positions. American Jesuit Virgil Blum attributes this to the country's latent, sometimes blatant, anti-Catholicism. But even were bias not a factor, staffers in key media positions normally judge a news story by the going standards of the trade which favor shock and controversy, and by American mores as well. These mores favor freedom over authority, democracy against hierarchy, this world over the next, utilitarian morality against any alleged "Word of God". The *New York Times,* the *Washington Post, Time, Newsweek,* CBS, with their pipeline to Catholic dissenters, have been powerful forces for shaping what Catholics think of their Church. During the papal funerals and John Paul's visit, for example, it came as no surprise that the media turned more often to the Richard McBriens, Sydney Callahans, Francis X. Murphys, Andrew Greeleys to explain Catholicism than to those supportive of papal teaching. Phil Donohue and Dick Cavett use their TV shows to caricature Catholicism in ways which bring outrage from media bosses if they used the same techniques to disparage Blacks or Jews. Even a quasi-serious journal like the *Atlantic Monthly* (May 1980) commissioned a report on the new Pope, which concluded with the advisory that John Paul II "has the opportunity to retrieve the disillusioned members of the Church" — if he is nice to Hans Kung and Edward Schillebeeckx.

The *New York Times* followed the news of John Paul's censure of Hans Kung with several op-ed disparagements of the Pope by Kung himself. Later still, when the *Times'* editor sought additional support for Kung he turned to Jesuit Walter Burghardt whose contribution ended up asking how we know what Catholic truth is. Bishops who stand up for the Church's doctrine are depicted in the American press as traditional, while problem bishops for the Vatican are presented as forward looking and enlightened. A partial reason why the bishops "ate crow" in 1967 (when they reversed themselves on the dismissal of Charles Curran from CUA) was their fear of how they would be made to appear in the media. In 1976 Archbishop Bernardin, after expressing outrage over presidential candidate Jimmy Carter's position on abortion, was also forced to "eat crow" at a press conference because the media men, egged on by a few of the Bishop's own staff, wished to build a case that Bernardin, then the president of *National Conference of Catholic Bishops* (NCCB), had shown too much favor to President Ford's and the Republican position on abortion. This did not please important members of the USCC staff, who were voting Democrats, as were the reporters doing the story.

On the other hand, the magisterium and its officers can no longer count on a square deal in the Catholic press, sometimes even in the media they own and pay for. There are "conservative" newspapers and magazines still, but the *National Catholic Register,* or the *Homiletic and Pastoral Review* are ridiculed or dismissed as trivial in professors' lecture halls and in many Church bureaucracies. *Commonweal, America, U.S. Catholic, Theological Studies, Chicago Studies* and the *National Catholic Reporter* are more respected by Catholic opinion-makers at first and second levels of Church influence. These organs, as everyone knows, point their articles and editorials toward positions rejected time and time again by the magisterium. Their heroes are customarily the sources of Catholic news for the secular press.

The change in the tone and content of the Catholic press is the result of the adoption since 1965 of secular publishing norms, often secular values. News for news' sake ("man bites dog") without regard for scandal or reputation has become a norm for some editors, without a second thought given to calumny and detraction, conduct which normally would be considered sinful. Material offensive to pious ears is published simply because it might appear in the secular press anyway. The image of "house organ" for the Church is to be shunned, even though the publications of prestigious secular institutions, established for the internal consumption of members, never think of allowing anyone to use these organs to denigrate or weaken the institutions which they serve. The *American Jewish Committee,* the *AFL-CIO,* the

Urban League value their survival too much to do so. Catholic editors not infrequently believe they enhance their secular reputations by disclaimers that the local bishop was involved in reviewing a story or an editorial. The *Catholic Press Association* (CPA) following its 1975 convention began to take dissent in the Catholic press for granted (*Origins*, Vol. 5, May 1975, p. 13). The CPA frequently gives awards (and therefore endorsement) to newspapers like the *National Catholic Reporter*, which regularly assails the magisterium, whose Catholicity was disavowed by its founding Bishop Charles Helmsing. Diocesan papers—actually intended to be the pastoral arm of the bishop—regularly feature columns which undercut the policies of the bishops and pope, or feed into the lives of the faithful discontent with things Catholic. One Catholic editor thinks it is now impossible to syndicate a news commentary or column which reflects the Church's official positions.

This reversal in Catholic communications came about mostly as a result of the activity of priests. Few noticed the change years ago when a magazine like *The Catechist* (January, 1968) had Fr. Robert Hunt (shortly to leave the priesthood) describe a new catechism to come out of Holland as "a Dutch treat". But by 1976 it was commonplace for *America* (July 10), seeking to explain the Dutch Church, to turn for "objective" reporting to ex-priest Peter Hebblethwaite who has little sympathy for Rome. The transformation in the editorial content of Catholic magazines has been remarkable. *Commonweal*, which in its first editorial professed its loyalty to the "presentation of orthodox religious principles" (12 November 1924), hardly takes any Catholic statement seriously if it does not meet secular (sometimes Protestant) standards. The "sure background" Michael Williams found in "the continuous, unbroken tradition and teachings of the historic Mother Church" has not been recognized as "sure" for many years in the editorial office of his successors.

America magazine from its earliest days (1909) up through the editorship of Thurston Davis, SJ, was reasonably (with few exceptions) "progressive" in the same sense that popes were—articulating the social gospel often better than *Commonweal* and more often than bishops, who prior to 1962 were not outstanding spokesmen for that particular gospel. During those days *America*, unlike *Commonweal*, was also staunchly Catholic on those moral values (mostly affecting family life) then under political attack in secular society. Beginning with the editorship of Fr. Donald Campion (and almost coinciding with the ill-fated move of Woodstock Theological College to New York) *America* was almost indistinguishable from *Commonweal*. The secular agenda became its own, whether the issue was sexual ethics, contraception, indissolubility of marriage, the ordination of women, or the nature of a Catholic university. *America's* Jesuits (today led by Fr. Joseph O'Hare) are now for the first time in the seventy year history of this magazine on "the other side" from Church authority. Not only is Rome wrong in many of her doctrinal positions, but it is responsible for making an "intellectual martyr" out of Hans Kung (11 March 1980) and its treatment of Edward Schillebeeckx is nothing short of a "scandal" (29 December 1979). One would be hard pressed in *America's* articles or book reviews to find doctrinal deviance treated objectively or critically. When the editors wished to discuss heresy they turned to Fr. Avery Dulles, Fr. Charles Curran, Fr. Richard A. McCormick, and Fr. Richard McBrien without embarrassment or pretense or even-handedness. *America*, once graced by the pens of Fr. Wilfred Parsons, Fr. Robert Hartnett, Fr. Vincent McCorry, Fr. Francis Canavan, and Fr. Benjamine Masse, has been freed of the magisterium's defenders much the same as *Theological Studies* dispensed with the services of Fr. John Ford, Fr. John Lynch and Fr. Joseph Farraher.

The Jesuits are not the only offenders, however. Maryknoll's press facilities have in recent years been devoted to revolution and Marxism, a trend symbolized best by the August 1980 issue of *Maryknoll* magazine with its roseate picture of Castro Cuba's good intentions and accomplishments. Another soft spot in the Catholic press, as far as orthodoxy is concerned, is the Paulist Press, once a great explainer and defender of things Catholic. The Paulist Fathers regularly publish books under their auspices which in normal times could not receive an imprimatur. The catalogue of the Paulist Press is a veritable "Who's Who in Dissent"—James Corriden, Raymond Brown, David O'Brien, Arlene Swidler, Walter Burghardt, James Young, Charles Curran, Richard McCormick, and a host of other revisionist writers. *Human Sexuality* is merely the most notorious Paulist publication. When the Paulist Press decided to disassociate itself from a second printing of that manuscript, its editor-in-chief sold the paperback rights to Doubleday, in spite of the book's condemnation by the Holy See and the American bishops, and seemingly without regard to its affect on the moral standards of Catholics.

Bernard Nathanson, author of the startling book *Aborting America*, once accused Doubleday's staff, mostly activists in the women's liberation movement, of sabotaging the promotion and distribution of his book because it honestly discloses the savagery of the abortion business. Doubleday executives exculpate their staff but admit that there is bias in bookstore management against Nathanson's kind of book—and against Catholic books such as *The Battle for the American Church*. Bias is found frequently in Catholic publishing houses as

well. A negative critique of Catholic teaching readily finds a publisher
and a market because it is considered new and saleable writing. A
defender of Catholic teaching finds few ready outlets even for good
writing. Fr. John C. Ford, SJ, for example, called upon all his prestige
in the Jesuit scholarly community to get his defense of the Church's
teaching on contraception into *Theological Studies* (June 1978). It was
accepted only on condition he would permit in the same issue an article on the same subject by a young dissenter. Publishers who print dissent regularly reject criticism of dissent in their publications.

A good example of the cynical mood of influential segments of the
Catholic press toward things Catholic can be found in the *U.S.
Catholic,* a slick magazine printed in Chicago. Awarded highest
honors for general excellence by the Associated Church Press in 1980,
this publication of the Claretian Fathers (whose staff at Louisiana State
University was dismissed by the Bishop of Baton Rouge for sundry deviance from Catholic norms and practice) takes pride in the new
Catholicism it allegedly represents. Their April 1981 issue, for example, responds to the question: "American Catholics: Just who do you
think you are?" with a series of articles suggesting that Catholics do
not have to be what normally the Church might expect them to be.
Managing editor Robert E. Burns debunks the pope and Sunday Mass
as the essential elements for describing what "makes a Catholic a
Catholic". Socialist David O'Brien, making Chicago priests his ex-
emplaries, wants to know who wrote a papal statement or who made a
chancery decision before either would be worthy of his acceptance.
Commonweal's John Garvey does not believe that patriotism or love of
America is a necessary element of being Catholic. Sr. Mary Ann
Walsh, RSM, describes Catholic conservatives as those living out of a
siege mentality or resisting Vatican II change by their preference for
the Baltimore Catechism, the Latin Mass, First Friday devotions etc.
America's editor Fr. Joseph O'Hare, writing under the rubric "you
ain't seen nothing yet," speaks with approval of selective disobedience
by future Catholics. Nowhere in the entire issue is there any reference
to "the obedience of faith" which Vatican II speaks of (*Verbum Dei*
No. 5), nor of the relationship of salvation to faith in the Word of God
as preached by the Church's priests (*Presbyterium Ordinis* No. 4), nor
that the Church is necessary for salvation (*Lumen Gentium* No. 14).
Instead, *U.S. Catholic* makes America's cultural pluralism the norm
for a doctrinal pluralism entirely inconsistent with Catholic faith.

Ten years have passed since the *National Catholic Reporter* first
celebrated the victory of "liberal" control of the Church's renewal (11
December 1970). Less than two years later *NCR* attributed that victory
in large part to "liberal" control of Catholic publications. *Concilium,*

the theological series now in its 100th volume, which began as a scholarly exposition of what Vatican II meant, today hardly refers to the Council at all—so far removed are prominent scholars from Catholic doctrinal positions. The diocesan press—using syndicated columns by theologians like Richard McBrien—dispenses counsel such as the following: "[too much has happened in the Church] to allow any Christian to justify his or her doctrinal positions merely by an appeal to the Bible and/or to the official teachings of the Church"; or, "You can be too loyal to the Pope. You can be too emphatic about the divinity of Christ" (*Brooklyn Tablet*, 9 October 1975, p. 25 and 12 April 1980, p. 2). The *Review for Religious* (1980/2, pp. 314-315) speaking of books on sexuality, would not recommend to a reader a strong defense of the Church's sexual ethic unless the reader at the same time took into account *Human Sexuality*, the book condemned by the Church. The "truth" ostensibly lies somewhere in between. The *Lectionary for Sunday Mass*, published by the Liturgical Press at Collegeville, Minnesota, offers a homily for the Seventh Sunday of the Easter Season which approves dissent, citing the conduct of Sr. Theresa Kane during the 1979 papal visit to the U.S. as a good example. The *Catholic Book Club* advertises Edward Schillebeeckx's *Jesus*, (which was under scrutiny in Rome for its dubious Catholic theology) as the Catholic book of the month.

The less direct, but not necessarily less effective, way of undercutting the magisterium under official auspices is to write an editorial in a diocesan newspaper granting Rome's rights but denying validity to Rome's conclusion. One editor, replying to the Holy See's declaration on sexual ethics, implied that Rome was not very clear-headed on premarital sex, homosexual activity, or masturbation. His concluding paragraph reads:

> To point to such flaws in an important document of serious ecclesiastical authority is to open oneself to the charge of disrespect. No disrespect is intended. We are deeply committed to the right and duty of ecclesiastical authority to teach the truth, but not to the presumption that ecclesiastical authority can create the truth. (*Brooklyn Tablet*, 12 June 1976).

Five years later this same editor pursued his course of undercutting the Church's teaching on contraception by presenting methods of family regulation as the free choice of Catholics as long as they are well intentioned. *Brooklyn Tablet* editor Don Zirkel invited Fr. Frederick Harrer to advise East Coast readers about the modern view on contraception (7 February 1981). Harrer writes of "personalist" morality as the new and right way of making Christian decisions: "Why a person does something is primary; the act itself and its circumstances are secondary." His readers are counselled to face sexual decisions with a developed "consciousness of insight", a quality of mind Harrer thought Paul VI lacked when he issued *Humanae Vitae*.

Perhaps the most noticeable change in the Catholic press since John Paul's arrival on the scene has been in *Our Sunday Visitor*. Under Fort Wayne's Bishop Leo Pursley (successor to founder Bishop John Noll) publisher Fr. Albert Nevins, MM, and editor Mr. Dale Francis, *OSV* became a highly successful publishing enterprise and a newspaper more widely circulated in Catholic parishes than any other in the U.S. Although Nevins was a known partisan of the Church's social doctrines, he was also quite orthodox about its creed and moral codes. During the turbulence following the late Council, Nevins and Francis together supported the magisterium, including Paul VI's *Humanae Vitae*. Dissenters, finding no support or compromise in this quarter, easily pinned the label "right wing" on anything *OSV* printed. Biting comments on its policies came from many quarters, including some within the United States Catholic Conference. "Left wing" criticism had little effect on *OSV's* circulation. Business actually improved.

When Chicago's auxiliary Bishop William McManus succeeded Pursley in 1976 questions arose immediately about how and when he would change the direction of *OSV* and about how long Francis and Nevins would last. Few observers expected things to follow in the Noll-Pursley mould. McManus, a close personal friend and associate of many Chicago dissenters, was also known to be opposed to Roman positions on religious education. Concerned observers did not have long to wait. Under criticism from McManus, Dale Francis resigned. In 1980 Fr. Nevins "retired". The new priest publisher brought in by McManus came from the Archdiocese of Chicago. Almost without delay Catholic dissenters, who formerly appeared on *OSV* pages only to be criticized, now began to be featured. New names, e.g. Edward Maron, appeared out of the East as a regular contributor. Maron is a pseudonym for a New York academic who has been fighting Romanism and clericalism since 1966. A Maron survey of Catholic morality in the United States (October 12 and 19, 1980) turned up the single conclusion that the important moral issues for American Catholics were social—war and peace, human rights, race and poverty. Parish priests and parish laity were probably surprised at Maron's results which he culled on behalf of *OSV* by asking the views of a half-dozen dissenting moral theologians, including two ex-priests. Little depth analysis was given to the views of the only orthodox moralist he did consult—John Connery, SJ, of Loyola University in Chicago.

When the new executive editor of *OSV*, Richard McMunn, introduced an op-ed page on November 16, 1980—a feature commonplace in secular newspapers wishing to demonstrate objectivity because their editorial slant is quietly accepted—his first chosen contributor was another Chicagoan—Joel Wells, former editor of *The Critic,* who for most of his years since Vatican II has opposed official Church policies and positions. Wells seized upon the opportunity afforded him to attack the Church's position on contraception as "arbitrary" and "outdated", suggesting also that the 1980 Synod of Bishops dealing with the family placed "further strain on the credibility of other church teachings, especially concerning divorce and abortion." *OSV* came under severe criticism from its readership for offering this platform to Wells, many of them sensing that the pulpit given Wells was distinguished, that the paper had seriously departed from its own traditions. *OSV* editors rushed to defend their new policy as an evenhanded effort to keep columns open to all points of view, even as they professed their intention to support the Church on the editorial page. The arguments they advanced in support of the new position did not prove to be convincing. *OSV* belatedly had adopted a policy first conceived during the Council by "closet" dissenters—e.g. by Notre Dame's Ave Maria Press of offering first only visibility for dissent without endorsement. That always came later.

In the meantime Fr. Nevins remains retired. Dale Francis moved on to the editorship of *The Catholic Standard,* the official newspaper of the Archdiocese of Washington. When Cardinal Baum moved to Rome, the new Archbishop James Hickey undertook to review Dale Francis' policies. What changes Hickey will initiate cannot at this point be determined. However, a recent news story has Dale Francis contracting with the *National Catholic Reporter* to "make its worldwide network of correspondents available to *The Standard.*" *NCR* has denied the authenticity of many major Catholic doctrines from its earliest days in Kansas City and was disowned very early by its founding Bishop Charles Helmsing as no longer really Catholic. It is strange now during the pontificate of John Paul II that *NCR* would be hired as a communication's adjunct to the archbishop responsible for the orthodoxy of The Catholic University of America. This small happening simply focuses attention on a very important question: Where do the bishops really stand?

Rome is asking the same question. On April 27, 1981 the Apostolic Delegate wrote every American bishop the following reminder:

Your Excellency:

With increasing frequency the Holy See receives letters from the United States complaining about articles appearing in Catholic newspapers, including diocesan publications, which cause harm to the Faith of the people because of lack of respect for the teaching and decisions of the magisterium. As you know, it is not unusual for such articles to contain criticisms and attacks even on the teaching authority and the person of the Holy Father. The impact of such criticism is heightened when columns are syndicated and widely circulated.

A letter from the Secretariat of State (March 31, 1981; Protocol No. 63408) expressed concern over this problem, and ordinaries are encouraged to consider their responsibilities in governing the policies of those publications over which they have control. To this I would add a word of encouragement for the promotion of a sound and vital Catholic press, so useful an instrument for evangelization and so vibrant in the life of the Church in the United States.

With cordial regards and every good wish, I remain,

> Sincerely yours in Christ,
> *Pio Laghi,* APOSTOLIC DELEGATE

The response by the Catholic Press Association to Archbishop Laghi is a measure of the contemporary problem. CPA officers objected to "the broad general nature of your criticism." They wanted instead specific criticisms direct to editors and columnists and suggested that the complaints made to Rome might have come from people who confuse dissent with discussion. The CPA reaction indicates how far this national association of Catholic pressmen has come to follow secular rules in dealing with truths of Catholic faith and how its present leadership is unlikely to fulfill the goal of Vatican II, viz., that the Catholic "press, whether it be established and directed by the ecclesiastical authorities or by individual Catholics, would have for its manifest purpose to form, to consolidate and to promote a public opinion in conformity with the natural law and with Catholic doctrines and directives" (Decree *Inter Mirifica* 4 December 1963, No. 14). An investigative commission is not necessary to establish how often this directive is violated in today's Catholic Press, some of which is owned by bishops.

Where Do the Bishops Stand?

3

If there is a fifth or a sixth segment of the American Church in tension with Rome it is likely to be found within the machinery of the United States bishops themselves—either in the bishops' Chancery Office called the United States Catholic Conference or in their own association now known as the National Conference of Catholic Bishops.

First, the *United States Catholic Conference*. The USCC is to the Catholic Bishops of the United States what the White House staff is to the country's President. Do we have there another example of a "little Holland" in the American Church? A good deal of evidence exists that we do. From the early post-Council days when USCC officials saw nothing wrong in calling the nation's family life directors together for a discussion of *Humanae Vitae* with Germain Grisez outlining the Catholic obligations contained therein, while Richard McCormick explained how the encyclical need not bind Catholic consciences, dissent has prevailed in high places in the bishops' machinery. In spite of the fact that, according to Archbishop Bernardin, the bishops' organization has "a responsibility for revealed truth" (*Origins* 24 May 1979, p. 5), it is not clear that USSC has honored that objective as an absolute priority at all times. USCC sometimes admits mistakes in its operations but the leadership there frequently covers up the distance that separates staff viewpoint from official church positions. Something admittedly is wrong when one reads such a headline as "Bishops Suppress Lay Author's Book" (on moral values) or "USCC destroys 2,000 books on sexism"—two of its own publications—because on the eve of distribution they were found to represent inadequately or distort Catholic doctrine. The second book was actually in print when USCC officials discovered its existence (*National Catholic Reporter,* 10 Oct.1975 and 27 April 1979). Nor is it easy to understand how a commentary on the *National Catechetical Directory* was to be written substantially by Catholic University of America's Fr. Berard Marthaler who initially was responsible for many of the early NCD difficulties and who thought the banned USCC book on sexism was "a careful study." What is even more surprising is that the bishop in charge of NCD's writing had no idea that Marthaler was to write a commentary, especially since he did not think NCD needed a commentary, and particularly if it explained the NCD away on the very points of orthodoxy about which the bishops were insistent.

Perhaps the way to approach the contemporary orientation of USCC is through an examination of *Origins,* the bishops' "Documentary Service." *Origins* was established to provide written materials which would assist Catholic leaders to understand what the Church proposed in the Second Vatican Council. It was patterned after the defunct *Herder's Correspondence,* which during Vatican II distributed pertinent commentaries on Council activity throughout the Catholic literary world. Herder's usually dispensed the most liberal interpretations of what was going on in Rome 1962-1965, reporting more of Holland's Bishop Bekker's explanation why contraception was permissible, than Cardinal Ottaviani's defense of Catholic doctrine on the same subject. *Herder's Correspondence* became the conduit through which Catholic academicians, out of touch with the daily doings in Rome, were led to expect the most radical change in the future Church from Vatican II.

Origins lacks such a simple one-sided bias for the reason that it publishes the official documents of the pope, of the Vatican Curia, the NCCB and individual bishops. But once this valuable service has been performed, *Origin's* editors are curiously selective in their choice of speeches and statements by non-bishops which they regularly publish with bishops' money. They almost always choose the statements of people who are known as Church critics or dissenters from the magisterium in one area or another. It is possible to conclude from reading these selections that official statements need not be the last word on the future directions of the Church. One rarely reads in *Origins* defenses of the magisterium against dissent nor serious criticism of dissenting positions. Throughout the six year period 1975-1980 (vols. 4-9), for example, *Origins'* editors revealed their favorite sources for viewpoints on American Catholicism. These non-episcopal sources were chiefly two:

Origins' Leading Catholic Organizations
They are (with the frequency of appearance in parentheses): Canon Law Society (5), Cara (3), Catholic Biblical Association, Catholic Press Association, Catholic Theological Society (2), Center for Concern,

Chicago Priests and Chicago Catholics, Leadership Conference of Women Religious or their individual spokeswomen (16), National Federation of Priest Councils (3), National Catholic Education Association, Women's Ordination Conference (2).

One would never know from *Origins* that there are Catholic organizations which disagree in whole or in part with opinions regularly expressed by the above organizations. The National Federation of Catholic Physicians' Guilds, the Consortium Perfectae Caritatis, the Institute on Religious Life, the *American Catholic Philosophy Association*, the Fellowship of Catholic Scholars, etc. are not recognized by *Origins* as articulating positions worth sharing with the Catholic world.

Origins published statements favoring the ordination of women by the Catholic Theological Society and the Catholic Biblical Association and an NCEA statement on the nature of Catholic Colleges which does not agree with John Paul II's view of what a Catholic college should be. *Origins* in that period *did not publish* statements favoring both Roman positions by The Fellowship of Catholic Scholars. (The Fellowship did not appear until 1981).

When addressing the problems of religious life *Origins* favored its readership with the views of Sr. Elizabeth Carroll, RSM, Sr. Mary Colgan, SSSF, Sr. Francis Borgia Rothluebber, SSSF, Sr. Margaret Brennan, IHM, Sr. Margaret Farley, RSM, Sr. Joan Chichester, OSB, Sr. Theresa Kane, RSM, all of whom are consistent antagonists of Rome. Not a word was cited from Sr. Mary Elise, SND, Sr. Joan Gormley, CND, Mother Claudia, IHM, Mother Bernadette Wiseman, PBVM, Sr. Mary Clare Hughes, SC, Mother Mary Sixtina, OSF, Sr. Bernadette Counihan, OSF—all of whom have made many statements on religious life in accordance with the documents of Vatican II and Paul VI.

Origins' Leading Catholic Opinion Moulders
The nationally known personalities featured by the USCC (1975-1980) for their views of Catholic life included Theodore Hesburgh, CSC (2), John Tracy Ellis (2), Andrew Greeley (2), David O'Brien (2), George Higgins (8), Timothy Healy, SJ, John Egan, John Noonan, Rosemary Haughton, James Coriden (2), Charles Curran (2), Avery Dulles (6), Hans Kung (4), Stephen Kelleher, Walter Burghardt, SJ, Joseph Cuneen, Raymond Goedert, Colman Barry, James Provost, Michael Warren, Raymond Potvin, Charles Whelan, James Young (4), Francis Buckley, SJ, Raymond Brown, SS, and the Berkeley theologians. This list of speakers and writers obviously is dominated by those closely associated with the Washington area of the Church (USCC and CUA), where a good deal of anti-magisterium sentiment is centered.

timent is centered.

During the six years covered by this study other things were going on in the Church and other things of importance were being said by Manuel Miguens, OFM, Mary L. T. Brown, John Hardon, SJ, John Kippley, John Sheets, SJ, William Smith, Herbert Ratner, MD, Germain Grisez and a host of other scholars and writers defending Church positions, sometimes with class and wit. But only once in all this period did *Origins* grace its pages with a thinker of this persuasion and this was James Hitchcock's short statement on moral values at a USCC bicentenial hearing (1976), certainly not one of his major critiques of contemporary American Catholicism. *Origins* did have space, however, for the apologias of three disciplined priests, Joseph O'Rourke, SJ, John McNeil, SJ, William Callahan, SJ. Paulist James Young regularly is displayed in *Origins*—a priest who travels around the country denying that Jesus uttered a divine mandate on the indissolubility of marriage, who openly predicts that the Church will bless the second marriages of divorced Catholics (*Commonweal*, 22 November 1974, pp. 187-196).

This freedom with which Fr. Young enters the pages of *Origins* is an additional symptom of bishops' ambiguous leadership on a Catholic problem more serious than the Church's difficulties over contraception. The unique moral teaching of Christ was the indissolubility of monogamous Christian marriage. It required almost 1500 years, the loss of England to the Church, the Council of Trent and the development of appropriate secular jurisprudence to institutionalize (at least in the West) this revelation in civil society, to say nothing of its acceptance by Catholics themselves. The modern secular state is now in the process of reversing the process, dismantling supports for the monogamous family and moving more and more towards the acceptance of polygamy, consensual sexual unions without benefit of marriage, and the substitution of state care (instead of family care) of children. The heartrending human situation of the increasing number of Catholics caught up in unhappy marriages created by secular social circumstances are too well known by pastors to need comment. Organizations like *The Judean Society* created to deal properly with the Christian difficulties which ensue from divorce never appear in the pages of *Origins* and are largely unpromoted by bishops. But the *North American Conference for Separated and Divorced Catholics* and its founder Fr. Young are featured not only by USCC but by individual bishops.

Pope John Paul II and Archbishop John Quinn, then president of the NCCB, both declared at the end of the 1980 Synod on the Family that invalidly remarried Catholics, while still members of the Church and welcome to the spiritual benefits of this membership, were ineligible as regular Eucharistic communicants. Yet Fr. Young, many diocesan officials, seminary professors, with the knowledge of bishops, are directing these Catholics to the altar rail on a massive scale. Onetime *NC News* reporter James Castelli's *What the Church is Doing for Divorced and Remarried Catholics* (Chicago: Clarentian Fathers Booklet, 1979) alleges that support of certain bishops and the NCCB's own *Committee on Pastoral Research and Practice* have encouraged the practice in spite of the Church's clear teaching. In effect, this intra-Church movement reinforces the secular trend of disestablishing the indissoluble monogamous sacramental marriage, as if the family unit derived from this precise marriage form has not enriched human lives and stabilized both State and Church for the past 500 years.

One of the peculiar stories to appear in *Origins* (8 March 1979, p. 2) was the myth that Pope John Paul I, had he lived, might have found a way out from under *Humanae Vitae*. *Origins* was silent that year on the binding statements of *Humanae Vitae*'s content, but did manage to disseminate the hoax about John Paul I through American Catholic circles. The veracity of the *NC News* story was denied by Cardinal Luciani's Vicar General in Venice and by Henri de Riedmatten, OP, secretary of Pope Paul's Birth Control Commission, both of whom said they would have known if that story was true. When an American theologian challenged *Origin*'s use of the editor's column to disseminate such a falsehood he was told: "The editorial content of *Origins* and of *NC News* is relatively independent of bishops' control." This alleged independence may explain why *NC News* in the judgment of many does not always provide coverage of Catholic events any more objectively than *Origins*. *NC News* sometimes has played down the unique political importance of the abortion issue, in part because the *NC* reporter assigned to this news story did not agree with the bishops' call for a constitutional amendment outlawing abortion.

USCC has also given uncertain signals on some important moral issues. Consider the question of contraceptive sterilization. In July 1980 the American bishops once again affirmed the traditional Catholic ban on contraceptive sterilization. USCC directives for Catholic hospitals had banned such surgical procedures as far back as 1971. This did not stop the spread of sterilization in those hospitals, however, because theologians, especially Richard McCormick, by justifying it for very serious reasons, encouraged groups like the Mercy Sisters, led by Sr. Theresa Kane, to authorize them in Mercy Hospitals. The American bishops, as if made uncertain by McCormick, raised the question about contraceptive sterilizations with Rome. Rome's answer came to NCCB on March 13, 1975 reinforcing the bishops' original position. For some strange reason, however, the Holy See's answer was never published until a year later when a doctor in London made it public at a meeting of Catholic physicians. Asked why the Roman letter was not publicized on time in the U.S., USCC's general secretary, the late Bishop James Rausch, explained that it was a "private response": "We saw no reason to make it public." The letter eventually appeared in *Origins,* June 10, 1976, but by this time religious communities had already expanded their sterilization services.

Liturgical abuses have also been treated cavalierly by USCC officialdom. One instance involved the making of Eucharistic Bread, which in some parts of the country was being confected with eggs and condiments (e.g. honey). Rubrics required that it be baked from a mixture of flour and water. Cardinal Franjo Seper informed Archbishop Quinn (June 4, 1979) that Masses celebrated with some of these concoctions were illicit, and at times even invalid. That directive did not impress the secretary to USCC's liturgical committee who told a pastor seven months later (February 21, 1980) that Seper's letter was "unacceptable". The Cardinal was not so easily put down because seven weeks later (April 17) Rome reaffirmed that Eucharistic bread be made only as directed, because it was a vital constituent of the sacrifice of the Mass.

USCC's inability or unwillingness to deal with the details of liturgical abuse or neglect is not of minor moment. The suppression of the Latin Liturgy in the U.S., the celebration of Mass without vestments or with profane readings, the decline in Benediction, Forty Hours' devotions, the non-use of penance before the Eucharist, the suppression of private confession in many parishes, the indiscriminate distribution of Holy Communion under both species and to non-Catholics, the common use of extraordinary ministers to distribute communion on Sundays and week days when priests are available and otherwise idle, have all been labeled abuses by John Paul II. These abuses were not uncommon in the American Church, especially in religious communities. The innovators, however, looked upon Vatican restrictions as evidence of Rome's narrow approach to liturgical reform. Encouraged by Archbishop Weakland, chairman of the Bishops' Committee on the Liturgy, diocesan directors began a letter writing campaign to Rome denying that such abuses existed. Cardinal James Knox's office (Congregation for the Sacraments and Divine Worship) did not take these assurances seriously because so many endorsements of American experiments came in stereotyped letters, and the evidence of selected abuse was too well documented.

The USCC staff rarely considered dissent one of the major problems of the Church. Msgr. George Higgins, USCC's veteran research director, once told twenty-year-old graduates of the Catholic University how good criticism and opposition is for the Church (*Origins*, 19 June 1980). His commencement address was understood by an *Our Sunday Visitor* commentator (3 August 1980) to mean that "Dissent isn't necessarily a Dirty Word." Yet dissent would be a "dirty word" for those who work for bishops in normal times. The word means denial of doctrine, sinful use of sacred persons, places and things (e.g. sacraments) sometimes the endorsement of immoral behavior. Dissent is different from disobedience, lack of discipline, violation of canon law, strange theological terminology, or unmannerly or vulgar accounts of things religious. Bad manners or bad behavior does not add up to bad faith. Dissent does mean bad faith. While USCC officials have never been accused of dissent in any personal way, there are occasions when confrontation with the magisterium over important doctrines has occurred within USCC offices. More commonly there is ample use in those offices of silences and practice of evasion about issues which bishops and popes treat with solemnity.

Deciding where to begin documenting these evasions of the magisterium is no easy task. A few examples may illustrate the scope of the problem:

- *An Introduction to Sharing the Light of Faith* published by the USCC (1980) leaves something to be desired as a summary of the *National Catechetical Directory*, even though this is its stated purpose. Those familiar with the history of *NCD* development remember how more than 100 amendments were needed on the floor of the 1977 Bishops' meeting to reintroduce into the document points of Catholic doctrine and practice which were poorly defined or omitted by the USCC staff in the drafting process between 1973-1977. USCC personnel almost immediately decided that the amended *NCD* (now known as *Sharing the Light of Faith*) needed a *Commentary* to be written by the very people responsible for the shortcomings bishops had found in the original *NCD*. Fearful that a *Commentary* might explain away the hierarchy's amendments, the bishop originally in charge of *NCD* asserted that there was no need for a *Commentary*. Although this declaration normally would have terminated the project, the USCC proceeded to draft an *Introduction* which appeared three years later as a *Summary* and which omits important phrasings incorporated as amendments by bishops during their 1977 meeting.

The following table illustrates some of the omissions: (The *italicized phrases* are especially significant.)

Item	Introduction	NCD
Creeds	"Ecclesial signs are those aspects of the Church's life besides liturgy, which include doctrinal or credal formulations..." (II c p. 3)	"Catechesis must nevertheless recognize credal statements and doctrinal formulas *as indispensable instruments for handing on the faith."* (Art. 47)
Hierarchy of Truths	"Catechesis...recognizes a certain hierarchy of truths; it is carried out under the guidance of the Magisterium of the Church." (II D p. 4)	"Hierarchy of truths does not mean that some truths pertain less to faith itself, but rather that some truths of faith enjoy a higher priority. The Bishop holds the primary position of authority over programs of Catechetics...The teaching of what is opposed to the faith of the Catholic Church, its doctrinal and moral positions its laws, discipline, and practice should in no way be countenanced in catechetical programs of any level." (Art. 47)
Faith	"Faith means assent, trust, surrender, and obedience—commitment—to God. In this sense, it is a deep personal relationship with the Lord." (III B. p. 7)	"The Act of Faith involves total adherence—under the influence of grace to God revealing himself. Total adherence—is a response of the whole person, *including belief in the content of revelation and of the Christian message."* (Art. 56)
Development of Doctrine	"Catechists need to understand the development of doctrine." (III c. p. 8)	After specifying three aspects for this development *NCD* concludes: "Catechists teach as authentic doctrines *only those truths which the magisterium teaches. When referring to speculative matters they identify them as such."* (Art. 60)
Ecumenism	"Catechists can foster ecumenism in a variety of ways (a) by clearly explaining Catholic doctrine..." (IV B p. 10)	NCD's line reads "explaining Catholic doctrine *in its entirety."* (Art. 76)

Item	Introduction	NCD
Infallibility	"The pope and the bishops... enjoy the gift of infallibility." (V E p. 14)	NCD adds for the pope: "even when he is not speaking *ex Cathedra* his teachings in matters of faith and morals demand religious submission of will and mind." (Art. 93)
The Church	"While working also to make the Church more faithful to Christ and its apostolic heritage, they (catechists) recognize that they can be enriched by the authentic insights of other religious traditions." (V E p. 4)	"Catholics are aware of *the uniqueness of the Catholic Church which possesses the fullness of the ordinary means of salvation—a fullness in which they desire all people to share.* At the same time, they also recognize that they can be enriched etc." (Art. 95)
Sin	(Neither defines original sin, nor does it mention or differentiate between mortal and venial sin.) (VG p. 15)	Art. 95 defines all three.
Conscience	"When people have become conscious of these fundamental goods and have cultivated an attitude of cherishing them, it is still necessary to decide how to realize and affirm them in concrete circumstances. Such decisions are called judgments of conscience. They must be based upon prayer, consultation, study, and on understanding of the teachings of the Church." (V H p. 16)	*The summary reflects NCD but omits the subsequent line: "One must have a rightly formed conscience and follow it."* (Art. 103)
Morality	Mentions Ten Commandments, Beatitudes, and Christ's Discourse at the Last Supper (V H p. 16)	*Introduction* omits works of Mercy, Virtues, Capital Sins, and Precepts of the Church (Art. 105

Item	Introduction	NCD
Eucharist	"The Eucharist increases charity within the visible community, is the chief source of diviniza- tion and maintains the pledge of immortality; is a memorial of the Lord's passion, death and Resurrection; is a holy meal which recalls the Lord's Supper, etc." (VI B p. 20)	*Ommited is the sentence of NCD (Art. 120) which reads: "This holy sacrifice is both a commemoration of a past event and a celebration of it here and now."*
Matrimony	"Catechesis—calls attention to the fact that openness to the procreation and education of children must always be pres- ent—includes a clear presenta- tion of the Church's teaching concerning moral methods of regulating births and the crime of abortion." (VI B p. 22)	Omitted is a phrase incor- porated in this paragraph by NCD (Art. 131): "A clear pres- entation of the Church's teach- ing concerning moral methods of regulating birth, *the evil of artificial birth control and of sterilization for that purpose and the crime of abortion.*"

Since the omitted and/or downplayed language of the *Introduction* represents some of the major contemporary controversies in Catholi- cism, with bishops on one side and dissenting theologians on the other, the question must be asked: How did the USCC come to publish a *Summary* which does not reflect *NCD* accurately? And if the *Introduction* is not a faithful summary to *NCD*, what explains the en- dorsement of the text by three bishops representing the National Con- ference of Catholic Bishops, which on page iii reads as follows: "In the judgment of the undersigned bishops, this document is in harmony with the text and spirit of the *National Catechetical Directory*. This document, therefore, can serve as a supplement to *Sharing the Light of Faith*."?

- *The Respect Life Booklet* published for 1978-1979 by the Bishops' Committee for Pro-Life Activities totally ignored the issue of contra- ception and its relationship to abortion. This in spite of *Humanae Vitae's* clear connection of the two. Furthermore, one invited con- tributor to that booklet was Fr. John L. Thomas, SJ, a notorious dissenter to that encyclical.

- The *National Conference of Diocesan Directors of Religious Education* produced a paper in 1980 entitled "Adults Making Responsible Moral Decisions" for catechists across the nation. Authored by Fr. Robert M. Friday, it is a veritable manual of how to divorce and remarry without public Church blessing and still have private Church approval from a priest acting on his own authority.

- After three years of input and numerous delays (due to concern that the text was not sufficiently Catholic) the USCC published in 1981 a booklet entitled *Education in Human Sexuality for Christians*. The guidelines contained therein are intended to assist Catholic parishes and schools to establish sex education courses for their young. Granted that sex education of any kind outside the home is a hornets' nest of controversy by itself, the USCC effort was defective from the beginning. The chosen committee was mostly composed of Johnny-come-latelys in the field of Catholic family life education, many of whom derived their practical experience during the period of dissent following Vatican II. Not a single nationally known figure from the scores who devoted long lives to the Catholic family apostolate (and to authentic sex education) appears on the Committee membership list. The finished product, therefore, leans heavily on contemporary sociological and psychological research rather than on Church documents. Since developmental psychology is already under fire in professional circles, it is likely that the USCC booklet will be criticized on this ground alone. More seriously, however, sexuality is repeatedly described in terms of personal self-enrichment much as the secular manuals do. Original sin, which was not mentioned at all in the first draft, works its way only into a footnote of the final copy (p. 10) and the word "concupiscence" does not appear at all, an element of Catholic belief about sexuality which colors all Church treatment of sexuality from the beginning of Christianity. Mortal and venial sins are never discussed, the intrinsic connection between sexuality and procreation is mentioned but not developed, the specifics of Church teachings are offered as positions not as truth, and offered without any substantial defense of why Church positions are true. The supernatural content of the document is almost nil, no absolute moral norms are ever inculcated, and in three places teachers are advised to introduce children ages twelve to fourteen to scientific knowledge about *all* methods of family planning (book's emphasis, pp. 85, 87, 88), not excluding contraception. There is no attempt to have the teacher motivate students to believe and hold what the Church teaches.

  Although approved by two bishops the book was published by the USSC without members of the Administrative Board reviewing its content or endorsing its publication."

- The USCC also has in process two other statements, on the sacrament of Penance, one to clergy/educators, one to the general public. The purpose of these documents is to revive among Catholics the practice of confession. The clergy/educators' statement is satisfactory but the one intended for the general public, while properly preoccupied with forgiveness, guilt and reconciliation, fails to come to grips with sin as human action, makes the gravity of sin a matter demanding an expert for its determination, and mortal sin to be a rare occurrence in the average person's life, diminishing the need for frequent confession. In speaking of the New Rite of Penance, the USCC draft does not emphasize the importance and priority of private confession or private absolution. In effect a USCC paper, intended to revive the use of the sacrament of penance, adopts as major operating principles the concepts which have eliminated confessional lines everywhere in the decade following Vatican II.

- Fr. Francis D. Kelly, an official of the *National Catholic Education Association* (NCEA) (which has a distinct but close relationship with USCC staff) recently said that religious educators were free to choose whether eight year old children should or should not receive first confession before first communion, arguing that "it is not obligatory to receive confession before communion" (*National Catholic Register* 8 March 1981). Kelly seized on the lax practices tolerated by the USCC encouraging disobedience to the discipline of the Holy See and the American bishops on first penance. Paul VI made it clear on March 31, 1977 that confession first is binding on the universal Church "except in cases which clearly called for exception". The *NCD* reads as follows (No. 126 p. 73): "The Sacrament of Reconciliation normally should be celebrated prior to the reception of communion." The end result of this continued disobedience by priests and religious is a generation of youth who do not go to confession in maturity. What is more dangerous to the future of the Church, youngsters do not know how to go to confession, even if they cared.

But one cannot hold Frank Kelly to account when bishops themselves are responsible for contradictory practice, some clearly in violation of Church regulation. Archbishop James Hickey found that postponed first confession has "children in high mobility areas missing first penance" so he reminded priests in Washington D.C. that *NCD*'s rule No. 126 (i.e. First Confession normally first) is to be followed in his diocese as "our constant pastoral practice". Contrariwise, the young Bishop of Rochester issued lengthy guidelines on the administration of the sacraments (many of which imposed new legal burdens on pastors in deciding who to baptize or marry) but failed to tell pastors that first penance normally comes before first eucharist, as *NCD* prescribes, a startling omission in view of the fact that Matthew Clark came to the episcopacy from Rome itself, where the Holy See's mind was clearly expressed more than once.

Members of the bishops' national staff seem at times to adopt as normative what is known as "the new theology" which explains why initial positions of the USCC staff—in all the cited areas—contraception, indissolubility, sexual ethics, Catholic universities, the sacrament of penance—are at odds with Catholic doctrine and/or administrative policies of the Church. Composers of those drafts do not take kindly to correction, as bishops discovered when they tried to correct the deviance in the early suggested texts of *The National Catechetical Directory*. Those bishops responsible for the final amendments to *NCD* had good reason to ask how these aberrations entered the USCC machinery in the first place.

This observation raises an important question. Where do the bishops find the staffs which create such problems? Repeated embarrassments ordinarily should lead bishops to review the make-up and source of the USCC personnel. They ordinarily might want to know why stalwart defenders of the magisterium seem to be excluded from participation in USCC's decision making process. The American bishops would have saved themselves a good deal of trouble back in 1970 when they chose six known critics of things episcopal to do research on the priesthood. Four of their scholarly selections later left the priesthood. The final reports in all four areas of research turned out to be biased in favor of the "scholars" own ecclesiastical preoccupations and were highly critical of the Church from a psychological, sociological and historical standpoint. The theological report on the priesthood was considered so un-Catholic that the bishops suppressed its publication. A report which said that Christ did not institute the priesthood was hardly complimentary to bishops. The bishops would have been better advised to hire six non-Catholics than rely on the Catholic scholars proposed by the USCC machinery.

The bishops did not learn a lesson from that experience. Critics continue to be their advisers. Appointees to USCC staff contain a disproportionate number of priests and laity educated under the aegis of dissenters. One bishop, finding a USCC committee oversubscribed with activists from the women's liberation movement, decided to offset this onesided influence on bishops' policy by suggesting the appointment of Phyllis Schlafly. He was informed that Phyllis Schlafly was unacceptable to USCC staff.

The mystery about USCC's ideological bent continues to deepen to this day. When in 1978 the USCC established a Commission on Marriage and Family Life to prepare a Pastoral Plan for the bishops, some curious appointments were made, not the least of which was Dr. William McCready, a dissenter from *Humanae Vitae*. Two years before this appointment, McCready (a collaborator of Andrew

Greeley), told a NCEA convention (*Origins,* 6 May 1976) that bishops ought to "withdraw from operational involvement in parochial school systems" and there should be a "total moratorium on official pronouncements about the do's and dont's of human sexuality". He denied that artificial contraception leads to disrespect for life: "What an underestimation of the sensibilities of so-called ordinary Catholic people!" he said. At this point McCready advised the Catholic teachers: "Why can we not assume that the Church too would grow and mature if it could admit that the rigid prohibition against artificial contraception was an honest mistake?" (This same researcher later denied he ever combatted the authentic teaching of the Church on contraception. [*Long Island Catholic,* 22 February 1979]) When McCready's membership on this commission was challenged, USCC leadership publicly defended the appointment on the ground that his research expertise, not his theology, mattered. Privately, however, the same leadership expressed surprise at his published opinions. If Dr. McCready's theology had nothing to do with the Pastoral Plan of Family Life, then it is more curious that this USCC publication ignored *Humanae Vitae*'s teaching on the integrity of the marriage act not only in the text, but in the documentary section. Sections 48, 49, 50 and 52 of *Gaudium et Spes,* which explicitly declares that Catholics "are forbidden to use methods (of birth regulation) disapproved by the teaching authority of the Church" were ommitted by the documentary section.

In preparation for the 1980 Synod of Bishops on the role of the Christian Family, *NC News* announced (12 May 1980) the following news item: "A theological consultation and symposium to prepare for this Fall's international Synod of Bishops in Rome will be held June 15-18 at the University of Notre Dame for Synod delegates from the United States and Canada." The agenda was planned by the USCC Commission on Marriage and Family Life and involved the American bishop delegates to that Synod. The bishops heard a report on Catholic families from Dr. William McCready's *National Opinion Research Center;* among the experts presenting papers were Fr. John L. Thomas, SJ, Sr. Margaret Farley, Fr. Richard A. McCormick, all dissenters. Not a single nationally known Catholic Family Life defender of *Humanae Vitae* was invited to participate, nor any of the activists in the apostolate of natural family planning or right-to-life. (This meeting at Notre Dame, and the ongoing participation in USCC affairs of contraceptive partisans such as Dr. McCready, Fr. Thomas, and Fr. McCormick explains in part Archbishop Quinn's initial presentation to that Synod.)

The customary excuse used by the chief officers of every institution in decline is to blame circumstances beyond their control or people down the line of their organization. James Hitchcock attributes the growing skepticism of Catholic laity to an avant-garde and iconoclastic Church bureaucracy, especially in Washington, D.C. If he is right, it may simply mean that priests sent to Washington to represent the Catholic cause eventually represent the secular culture of the nation's capitol or stand more for the professional interests of their particular specialties than those of the Church. It can also mean that bishops are poor choosers of sub-alterns or poor managers of institutions over which they have absolute control—at least theoretically. In such a situation the problem of the Church would be the body of bishops itself.

During Paul VI's pontificate irresponsible scholars were sometimes blamed for the Church's problems. Bishops then justified their vacillation toward the problems scholars created on the "Hamlet" in Rome. Eventually scholars' action and bishops' inaction worked out long term negative effects on the Church body. Recently, however, things have begun to change. Dissenting scholars are facing serious criticism within their own ranks, a development which in theory at least is supposed to restore scholarly balance and some semblance of intellectual order to the Church. Yet ecclesiastical peace is not coming. Criticized or not, dissenters have not been displaced from the privileged position they now hold in the Church. Nor do they give any indication of ceasing their disruptive activity in Catholic centers of learning or in the press. They act as if they were the men of authority. They inflict academic punishment on defenders of the magisterium—in publications, promotions, tenure, in reputation, penalties which few academicians endure with comfort. The price for challenging dissenters in power is to be put down either as a Neanderthal type or as an anti-Vatican II fundamentalist, or to find oneself out of work.

The central question for the Church, however, may no longer be what scholars are doing to harm the faith, but what bishops are doing to prevent irresponsible scholars from harming the faith. The issue is not scholars' right to freedom but how bishops deal with scholars who abuse freedom. Pope John Paul II seems to be taking well-orchestrated steps to assert his authority over scholars. Are the American bishops doing anything to exercise their authority over scholars?

The American bishop has little difficulty suspending a priest who violates Church norms by saying the Tridentine Mass. The body of bishops also has little difficulty persuading a well-disposed priest to desist from creating a pastoral problem. This it did when Fr. John Dedek (a protégé of Charles Curran) was returned to his Chicago archdiocese rather than fight for tenure at Catholic University of America.

Bishops also have little difficulty isolating or denying official position to so-call rightists. *Time* once reported how Catholic bishops wielded hierarchical clout against "the right" which they once reserved for "the left" (8 July 1974). However, disciplining obstreperous dissenters is so painful to bishops that it hardly occurs at all. It is this timidity which encourages some dissenters to believe that bishops will eventually legitimate dissent. At least they expect Catholic theory to catch up in time with the Catholic practice dissenters now institutionalize *ex lex*.

It is not easy, therefore, to be a bishop in a virulently anti-authoritarian period of history. Nonetheless, it is strange for bishops to be receptive to dissenters and cool to the orthodox teachers of the Church. The average bishop faces lowered Mass attendance, empty confessional boxes, declining schools, alienation among Catholic youth, evidence of alarming incidence of moral corruption among his faithful (higher than anything experienced by his predecessors) and evidence of disbelief in Catholic doctrines about Jesus, Mary, the pope, eternal life and a revealed morality. He also has priests teaching different doctrines in neighboring parishes or dioceses, nuns moving through his diocese detached from religious community life, scarcely known often to the pastors in whose parish they function. If his diocese has a college and university he can be sure that the young Catholics there (the faithful with whom his successors must deal) are being taught different things in different classrooms about Christianity and the Church. Sometimes they are being taught to disrespect the Church, if not to doubt the substance of the faith. He has a good seminary or he does not, but if he lacks one, he is not sure where to send his aspiring priests for a solid orthodox formation in Catholic truth and disciplined life.

These conditions did not result from anything conservative Catholic thinkers or preachers have said or done. Unless the bishop considers the present conditions an improvement over what he was bequeathed by his predecessors, one wonders why he is afraid to be a conservator of what is peculiarly and truly Catholic. Why is he not defending those values and practices to which so many of his predecessors devoted their energies and their lives? Or, does he think that new ministries, charismatic activity, ecumenical openness and new social awareness—all clear and profitable Post-Vatican II gains—are adequate compensations for broken faith and broken discipline, that these represent the intentions of John XXIII when he convoked the Council?

The average bishops' problem is compounded by the public relations nomenclature of contemporary culture. Traditionalists are those with nostalgia for the past, progressives are those leading the Church to new understandings; right-wing Catholics resist Vatican II changes, left-wing Catholics fashioned the documents of the Council and are the best guides to its implementation; conservatives are wedded to one theological method or one liturgical expression or one historical period, liberals are engaged in reconciling old Catholic formulas and institutions to modern science, modern philosophy, modern democracy, modern humanism. In the battle of words even bishops are persuaded that the balance of favor is on the side of "progress", "left wing", "liberal". These favorite words of secular (as against sacred) society represent the tendency, born of historicism, to break with absolutes of any kind. Problem solving in contemporary society tends to avoid abstract principles and to divide competing claims down the middle. The useful is good, the practical is good, the popular is good, change is good, the mainstream is good, etc. Such pragmatism has much to recommend it to a society which acknowledges no revelation, no natural law, no divine judgment. However, pragmatism begets its own social disorder. A modern politician who chooses to be practical tends to compromise against the public good, if only to gain or keep the perquisites and power of office-holding. Under his political cover power brokers with specific goals in mind harness society's vested interests and political power on behalf of their private agenda. The alleged "political moderate", to keep power or "peace", makes concessions which lower the quality of life or the social standards of the community. He seeks a broad political base which becomes so broad that social disarray is inevitable. At a given point the officeholder normally responsible for directing society toward its established goals finds himself incapable of achieving those objectives.

Secular officeholders tend to swim with this tide of current events rather than make their own history. They prefer to conform to people's wishes or at least to the wishes of seemingly political activists rather than to chart heroic courses in the people's best interests. American leadership is not known for high levels of inspiration and performance. "The brightest and the best" seemingly do not aspire to office-holding with traditional enthusiasm. The reason John Paul II electrifies the secular, as well as the Catholic world, is due in part to his obvious charismatic and ruling qualities. But he also walks tall because the society and Church in which he functions is no longer graced with Roosevelts, DeGaulles, Churchills, Pacellis or Stepinacs.

Catholic bishops have a trying role to play in this difficult situation. They do not need lessons on how to balance competing interests, how to be of service, how to please. They are as agreeable a body of men as ever held office in the American Church. One would be hard put to name a task-master among them or a curmudgeon as might have dominated Church history in the 19th century. The new president of the NCCB, Archbishop John R. Roach of St. Paul, when asked what he was going to do about growing dissent replied wryly, "I haven't ordered a public whipping for a long time" (*New York Times*, 11 November 1980, p. A16).

However, the colorful "characters" in the hierarchy of a generation or two ago had one advantage over modern bishops: as outsiders in a Protestant culture, they did not have to worry about popularity or acceptance. They could proclaim their faith even if it annoyed native Americans, confident that they were rallying points for Catholics. Today, however, bishops have social status of a different kind. They are integrated leaders within the American community, which is more homogenous than it once was, wedded more to civil religion than to confessional bodies. The Catholic community itself has been secularized and is comfortable with bishops who follow the leadership-style in modern society. It no longer is one in its beliefs, nor disposed anymore to rally around bishops simply because they are bishops. Yet Catholic bishops cannot be servile conformists. They are the chief witnesses to a revelation from God. They represent a distinct tradition in Christianity and function under Church law like every Catholic, including the authority of the pope. What secular society considers "progress" may not represent progress for the Church. Contemporary society at the moment lays great stress, for example, on sexual expression as a basic right and a necessary constituent of human happiness. Is not this a regression to the condition of the world when the Church first appeared? Is not Christian progress and moral development associated instead with marriage, moral law and virtue? The bishop's mainstream is marked out by the teaching of the Church, not by the going mores. A bishop need not enforce every expectation or law of the Church. This would be an impossible task, considering the varieties of Catholics in his diocese. Catholics were once called *nuclear* when they observed most of the rules while actively working for the Church; *modal* when they observed most of the rules without actively engaging in Catholic works; *dormant* (i.e. sleepers) if they maintained Catholic identity but did not participate in the sacramental life of the Church; and *apostate* if they abandoned Catholicism.

Perhaps thirty to fifty percent of all baptized Catholics today are dormant or apostate, for whose welfare bishops must manifest appropriate solicitude. However, unlike their secular peers bishops cannot seek reconciliation with them by splitting differences about life style. They may tolerate deviance, but not everywhere nor on all subjects. In other words, the beliefs and standards of dormants and apostates cannot become norms for Catholic life or reasons for muting the full intent of Catholic doctrine. In fact, there are times when bishops in conscience must condemn persons, places or things which suborn the faith or threaten the Church.

Some bishops have failed in recent years to protect their people's faith by acquiescing in developments which cannot be justified under existing Church law or sound norms of pastoral care. They have lowered standards to keep peace. How the Church is compromised by the poor judgment of bishops can be illustrated without difficulty. The surprising thing is that some of these episcopal responses continued to be made after the accession of John Paul II to the papacy and when it should have been clear that the future of the Church was being chartered in other directions.

- When Bishop William Hughes, one-time executive board member of the *National Federation of Priest Councils,* came to the See of Covington in 1979 he introduced his priests early to the theology of Fr. Richard McBrien—a complete reversal of the policy of his immediate predecessor. McBrien considers Catholicism to be the most respectable sect within Christianity but his theology would not equate the Catholic Church with the Church of Christ. Hughes also inherited St. Pius X Seminary in Erlanger, Ky., which was described a few years earlier as "crowded beyond full capacity". He proceeded to dismiss (without hearing) three of the faculty there because they were not "in the mainstream of contemporary theology." All were solid supporters of the magisterium. One of those dismissed was Jesuit moralist Fr. Thomas O'Donnell the main author of the NCCB's 1971 *Ethical and Religious Directives for Catholic Health Facilities,* and well known for being in the mainstream of John Paul II's moral theology.

- Archbishop Rembert Weakland has made a number of unusual judgments since becoming Milwaukee's ordinary (1977). His Religious Education Office (with his permission) sponsored a program for diocesan catechists in 1979 which featured Charles Curran. The justification for this appearance was Curran's good standing at Catholic University of America. In the same year a new auxiliary, having professed his acceptance of the Church's position on the ordination of women, recanted his fidelity to that teaching immediately after being made a bishop (*Milwaukee Sentinel,* 26 December 1979). In 1980 Weakland, chairman of the Bishops' Committee on the Liturgy, publicly confessed (*Our Sunday Visitor,* 31 August 1980) that contrary to liturgical norms at that time he has been tampering with the words of consecration at Mass (excluding the sexist phrase "for men"). Not long before this confession of fault the Archbishop excoriated the editor of the *Social Justice Review* (10 July 1980) for disloyalty to bishops by merely reporting two news items: "Pope Hears Confessions on Good Friday"—"American Bishop Stops Confessions on Good Friday."

The *Milwaukee Journal* (9 November 1980) tells the story of a workshop weekend on nontraditional families organized the week before by Greg Ward and Andrew Graff. This was part of the Midwest Lesbian and Gay Communications Network Conference. Ward defined "family" in terms of what people do, not what they are. "Sharing", he said, is what makes family life. His partner Graff believes that "people are adapting to different concepts of family." Ward and Graff, both activists in *Dignity,* the Catholic homosexual organization, are also members of Archbishop Weakland's Archdiocesan Commission for the Plan of Pastoral Action for Family Ministry.

On June 1, 1981 *The Milwaukee Sentinel* began a series on homosexuality among the clergy with a special reference to the thirty homosexual Catholic priests in Wisconsin (out of the total forty-five interviewed). The *Sentinel* reporters indicated that homosexuality among priests, ministers and rabbis is now a national problem, one not confined to a particular region of the country. Although the *Sentinel* held this story back for several weeks unsure apparently how to deal with a serious "sin" pattern developing among one of the most admired bodies of men in American society. Archbishop Weakland's compassion for homosexuals is recognized by *The Sentinel* but Weakland's earlier comment on the subject in his diocesan newspaper hardly gives evidence of any determination to eradicate the evil itself. In the Archbishop's July 18, 1980 column in *The Catholic Herald Citizen* Weakland, after weakening the meaning of biblical statements on the subject, (he calls St. Paul "harsh" on heterosexuals who commit homosexual acts) goes on to tell his people: "Current Church teaching which we Catholics must adhere to expects gay people to remain celibate, a position which is difficult for them to accept, but, frankly, one which I cannot sidestep." Such a statement in its inflexion and content hardly reflects the firm Catholic teaching one expects from a Catholic bishop.

• Archbishop Raymond G. Hunthausen in Seattle has also achieved a certain prominence in recent years by granting an *imprimatur* (a guarantee that the book is free from doctrinal error) to Sulpician Philip Keane's *Sexual Morality: A Catholic Perspective* (New York: Paulist Press, 1977), although the book is replete with errors. Hunthausen's diocesan newspaper published a recipe for Eucharist Bread which not only was clearly in violation of Vatican norms, but, if fully implemented, rendered invalid the Masses said with such "bread". A *Seattle Times* article on Hunthausen (July 12th), sparked a complaint from a mother about the postponement of infant baptism in one of his parishes (in favor of a catechumenate which would delay baptism "even into adulthood"). Hunthausen's school office also denied approval to religious education texts published by the Daughters of St. Paul and *Our Sunday Visitor.*

- Auxiliary Bishop Thomas Gumbleton of Detroit publicly announced his reservations about the Vatican's procedures in dealing with Hans Kung, indicating that Kung should better be evaluated by his peers (*Religious News Service,* 9 April, 1980).

- Archbishop John J. May, who has made some fine statements once he settled into St. Louis, began his ministry with confused reactions to issues with important doctrinal overtones. He defended the right of St. Louis University to invite Charles Curran to lecture, although he did not favor Curran addressing his ordinary St. Louis Catholics. May thought that Curran "has taken some controversial positions in recent years" but implied that the theologian's critics have not read his books (a statement that falls short of being factual since some of the complainers were scholars themselves). Although every local bishop is commissioned to be the protector of the faith in his own diocese, May prefers that the judgment on Curran be left to Rome (*St. Louis Review,* 4 April 1980). Curran returned May's compliment by telling his St. Louis audience that the moral doctrines of the Church were peripheral to the faith. Later, the new Archbishop called an anti-abortion protest involving trespassing "ill-advised and counter-productive", even as he alleged other protests in civil rights matters were not (*St. Louis Post Dispatch,* 18 April, 1980).

  Another indication of how May approaches matters of Catholic doctrine is his creation of a sixty-four member Archdiocesan Commission on Evangelization. The only theologian members are Dr. Laurence J. O'Connell, Chairman of the Theology Department at St. Louis University, and Fr. Ronald Modras, a Detroit priest brought by O'Connell to St. Louis University's theological faculty. O'Connell, the man responsible for the aforementioned lecture there by Charles Curran, told the new commission members that three factors were involved in theological reflection on the evangelization process: Sacred Scripture, culture, and personal experience. Significantly, his report did not mention the magisterium, although the Church's teaching is central to any truly Ctholic evangelization process. Lapsed Catholics or Americans of little or no religious faith at some point must accept this teaching if they are to be considered truly evangelized. Fr. Modras was one of the five-member committee which composed the CTSA report called *Human Sexuality,* a study of which was criticized by Rome and the American Bishops.

- Bishop James P. Lyke was interviewed by the *New York Times* on the occasion of his episcopal ordination as auxiliary to Bishop James Hickey (then of Cleveland). Lyke, a young Black man of 40, expressed the view that bishops are more enslaved than blacks: "They think there is only one way of looking at the world, one theology, one set of sexual standards. At least in the ghetto I'm from, we accept people as they are." Citing a disparity between the sexual morality of many blacks and the official teachings of the Church on birth control and extramarital sex, Lyke thought the Church needed "creative pastors" who could respect the black experience. Lyke found he could not bring many of his people into the Church because they were living in sin (*New York Times,* 2 August 1979).

- Bishop Joseph V. Sullivan of Baton Rouge became a beleaguered bishop when he denied Charles Curran the use of a diocesan facility for a lecture. Not only was he criticized by Apostolic Delegate Jean Jadot, but not a single bishop offered him public support when he removed the Claretian Fathers (who invited Curran) from their campus ministry posts at Louisiana State University (where Curran was to speak) although many showered him with private words of encouragement.
- About the very time that Rome issued a document reminding bishops of the importance of infant baptism, the Archdiocese of Newark was issuing proposed guidelines which intended to "limit the occasions when baptism will be administered to perhaps six times a year" (Newark *Advocate,* 19 November 1980, p. 3).
- Bishop William McManus of Fort Wayne, *ex officio* chairman of the board of *Our Sunday Visitor,* proposes as possibly legitimate the view that "there could be situations in which the value of marriage itself might take precedence over the good value of performing the marital act in the normal fashion" (*OSV* 22 February 1981). He articulated a proportionalist theory of morality, which in essence says that something basically wrong may be justified for a proportionately grave reason. Under this theory the customary moral demands of Christian faith become ideals or counsel of perfection, not requirements binding under pain of sin. The Holy See and the American bishops have rejected proportionalism as applied to sexual matters more than once. Subsequently, McManus chided the *OSV* editor (1 March, 1981) for publishing his private views. (*Our Sunday Visitor* is the largest circulation Catholic newspaper in the United States.)

About the time Bishop McManus gave Catholic married couples (and implicitly other Catholics) a dispensation from Catholic sexual norms, Pope John Paul II was speaking to the families of the Philippine Islands (February 19, 1981) about contraception. Said the Pope to the poor of those impoverished islands: "The Church will never dilute or change her teaching on marriage and the family." The Pope made very clear what the Church stands for in these matters: "On my part I owe it to my Apostolic Office to reaffirm as clearly and as strongly as possible what the Church of Christ teaches in this respect, and to reiterate vigorously her condemnation of artificial contraception and abortion" (English *L'Osservatore Romano,* 2 March 1981, p. 5). Last October 25th the Pope spoke to the Synod of Bishops on the "Duties of the Christian Family in the Modern World", agreeing with the world's episcopal delegates that God's Law is not "merely an ideal to be achieved in the future" but rather "a mandate of Christ the Lord that difficulties constantly be overcome."

What Bishop McManus was proposing belatedly in the history of Catholicism, and what the Pope was rejecting, is a moral norm that the end justified the means, that evil can be done if good is accomplished, that vice now can be looked upon as virtue.

Perhaps of greater concern is the fact that McManus claims to have acquired his new moral theology at a meeting of bishops. During the period February 2-6, 1980, 200 bishops travelled to Dallas to learn from "scholars" what marriage and sexuality mean (according to McManus) "in the light of magisterial teaching and the Christian theology of the person". If the Texas meeting impressed the Fort Wayne bishop as he said it did, one is inclined to ask: Why would 200 bishops travel to Texas to hear "scholars" unknown to them, to expose themselves to "teachers", not one of whom had published a major work in his own field, to hear a defender of "proportionalism" without hearing also from a leading representative of the Church's theological tradition which, according to the magisterium, is based on God's revelation.

The workshop's sponsor — Pope John XXIII Medical-Moral Center in St. Louis — asserted its intent to "balance" the presentations but the secular press and some bishops sensed instead an effort being made to soften the bishops' doctrinal positions or at least to develop a "pastoral approach" within the Church which would recognize the legitimacy of sexual life styles contrary to what bishops were bound "officially" to teach. The St. Louis *Post-Dispatch,* which had access to the Center's 250 page book *Human Sexuality and Personhood,* a collection of the talks intended for distribution through Catholic book stores, saw the Dallas meeting as an effort "to bring the bishops up-to-date on the latest research and thought" on sexuality (27 February 1981).

The viewpoints which made their way (from the assigned talks) through the Catholic media to the faithful suggested that men and women are "incomplete as human beings" without the other sex and "need the other to find completion through affective union with those of the opposite sex" (Fr. Ambrose McNicholl, OP). A number of speakers maintained that the primary role of sexual union is "enabling the person to reach fulfillment." Not only McNicholl but Fr. John Gallagher, whose task was to review magisterial teaching, pointed out that the "essential orientation" of sex and marriage is not an automatically accepted principle among Catholic theologians today. He suggested that "demands of situations" may justify exceptions to the rules of sexual ethics, including use of artificial contraceptives. "Why may we not appeal to the total good of the marriage, to other values in a situation, to allow artificial contraception in particular cases, at least as the lesser of two evils?" he asked. Fr. Benedict M. Ashley, OP, to justify revised sexual norms, used as his supporting authority the book *Human Sexuality,* which was denounced by the American bishops as late as 1977. The lecture on "proportionalism" — which the sponsoring Center planned as an even-handed presentation of the pros and cons — ended as a back-door endorsement of its use in decision-making about contraception. Although the Church's moral dictum on contraception was the backdrop against which all speakers approach their subject matter, the real issue at stake is far greater: Were there really any absolute Christian norms at all relative to sexual behavior? Traditional condemnations by the Church of fornication, adultery, homosexual activity, even bestiality, are being relativized, if not so directly as the norm governing the use of contraception.

The shortfall of Dallas is already evident in the McManus interview with *OSV.* The long-term results are not predictable at this time, although guardians of the Church's ancient norms for Christian behavior in sexual and other areas of life historically have been predictable in the firmness of their teaching. One thing is certain: the voice of Dallas is already being heard around the Church of the United States. Within a month of its completion *America* magazine (7 March 1981) featured an article, "An End to the Birth Control Controversy?" How is that to be done? By legitimizing the use of contraceptives after the manner suggested by Bishop McManus.

Individual bishops doing and saying strange things are one thing, the activity of the president of the National Conference of Catholic Bishops is quite another. NCCB, the creature of Vatican II, has been ineffective in dealing with dissent, even as it widened and deepened in the Catholic community. With each triennial change of NCCB's presiding officers the question is asked anew: What is the organized body of bishops prepared to do about the heterodox teaching rampant in Catholic institutions? The record indicates the answer to be little, if anything. Apparently the bishops operate on the principle that patient sufferance and friendship with dissenters would over the long run ease, if not solve, the problem. Actually, patient dealing has only widened and deepened dissent. In 1977 a more positive approach was envisaged with the election of Archbishop John R. Quinn as NCCB president. Quinn,a prime defender of *Humanae Vitae* in 1968, on his election listed the papacy as Catholicism's first and foremost resource "in saving the faith and the Church." Three years later at a press conference (May 1980) Quinn announced as Church policy that neither he or other bishops planned to "speak out" about Charles Curran (*National Catholic Register* 18 May 1980).

The issue, of course, no longer is inaction about dissent over contraception, but closed episcopal eyes to a wide range of false or distorted doctrines regularly inculcated in institutions for whose Catholicity bishops are ultimately responsible. The implications of Quinn's response at that press conference are inescapable. Episcopal toleration of false teaching legitimizes that teaching and *ipso facto* legitimizes Catholic lives organized around those opinions. In practice, it makes Catholic teaching on important religious matters, some of it allegedly revealed, a dead letter.

The teaching authority of NCCB was further compromised by Archbishop Quinn in his opening address in Rome (September 29, 1980) to the Synod of Bishops on the Family. He alleged later that the press misquoted and distorted that message, but the text itself was an unusual presentation for a bishop, one open to the very explications made by the world-wide press: "U.S. Bishops Challenge Pope" (*Chicago Tribune*), "U.S. Bishops Urging Rome to Reexamine Birth Control Issue" (New York *Times*), "Open Birth Control Debate" (*Washington Star*), "Ask Contraceptive Review" (*National Catholic Reporter*) Not surprisingly the Francis X. Murphys, Andrew Greeleys, Jim Castellis of the Church leaped on the statement to hail what seemed to be a challenge to *Humanae Vitae's* strictures. The Archbishop of San Francisco may have meant to convey perfectly proper concepts but the dangerous implications of the talk were seen within USCC prior to his presentation. After the fact, some bishops felt impelled to telex the Pope immediately rejecting and repudiating what Quinn said.

The question here is not the NCCB president's intention or his personal orthodoxy, but his judgment as chief officer of the magisterium in the United States. Almost immediately after *Humanae Vitae* (1969) Quinn identified that teaching as "bound up with the deposit of faith." His personal and official position on this subject has not changed. He reaffirmed his acceptance of that teaching in the opening lines of his Rome address.

It was the remainder of that address which confounded his worldwide audience. If he only meant to say the Church needs to develop a better rationale and catechesis for the teaching, then the text was ill-conceived and badly structured. The address requires critical comment because it symbolizes what is wrong with the NCCB's approach to the Church's contemporary doctrinal problems.

Archbishop Quinn could have saved himself and the Church a lot of trouble had he said in his Synod talk what he later said by way of clarification—once he saw the newspaper headlines. In a series of subsequent Roman press meetings and/or releases Quinn expressed the following opinions: Catholics who use contraceptives commit sin; contraception is related to growing rates of divorce and abortion; we should promote natural family planning; "liberal" Catholics should accept the Church's teaching on contraception; dissenters cause doubts about many Catholic teachings and go beyond Vatican II. Not one of these later assertions was part of his Synod address.

What precisely was wrong with Quinn's talk?

His reach for a "fourth way" to deal with *Humanae Vitae* (neither silence, repetition of past formulas, nor dissent) had the flavor of the subterfuge dissenters themselves used since 1963 to bypass the Church's clear teaching to deny the doctrinal principle without changing the language. Some of Quinn's paragraphs explaining his thinking contained the following language: "It is not a complete treatment", "The church has always recognized the principle and fact of doctrinal development", "Are there nuances and clarifications, further considerations and greater pastoral insights still to be elaborated?" Insinuating new possibilities of selective use of contraception while professing fidelity to the Church's general principles was developed to a fine art by Bernard Haring (1962-1968), and subsequently by Charles Curran, Richard McCormick and the school of moral theology which follows their lead. Reports familiar with these tactics of dissent can be excused for suspecting that Quinn was moving in the same direction, even though factually he was not.

His presentation of data on the extent of the contemporary Catholic problem relied totally on Andrew Greeley and William McCready (dissent among 76.5 percent of Catholic women, 71 percent of priests). But he made no reference to the bishops' role in the spread of that dissidence from 1963 onward, and his acknowledgement that contraceptive activists are people "whose learning, faith, discretion and dedication are beyond doubt" hardly takes into account that segment of contraceptive activism which is less than charitable toward pope and bishops, to put it mildly. Quinn's ingratiating words for opponents of Catholic doctrine left the bottom line to Catholic teaching on this subject vague and uncertain.

His explanation of the context of the problem—the world's demographic problem—has been rejected by the Holy See more than once at international meetings. This framework seems to suggest to Catholics that "responsible parenthood" means no more children than the demographic situation allows, a point of view actively promoted by the International Planned Parenthood Federation for more than a generation.

His proposal that "dialogue with theologians" will alleviate the Church's problems over doctrinal matters is naive — in view of his own experience with dissenters. These theologians have used "dialogue" as a professional technique for avoiding authoritative episcopal decisions in the hope even of bringing bishops over to their side. Delays afford them time to proliferate more widely their private dispensations of Catholics from bishops' norms. As the Synod of Bishops finished its business in Rome, a Washington colloquium of bishops with theologians (October 23-25) was beginning. During this latter meeting bishops were informed during the dialogue that there are only a few *de fide* definitions that it is the responsibility of theologians and biblical scholars to articulate just what the faith means for contemporary man. Quinn's suggestion at this late date, therefore, that the Holy See "listen" to dissenting theologians (a century-old position developed by Modernists as a tactic to convert Rome) may be the clearest example of his naiveté. Rome has listened to them repeatedly and having listened has rejected their view of revelation and moral law. Quinn, setting himself against the Roman experience, reveals the key reason why American bishops have been a total failure in dealing with dissenters.

The Quinn Synod address symbolized all that is wrong with episcopal leadership in the United States — if the Holy See's principled response to dissent is normative. The formulation of the Roman position began in the middle years of Paul VI's pontificate and is not peculiar to John Paul II. While the one-time NCCB president deplores the consequences of dissent, his Synod address did not attack dissent per se, as the Popes have done. Neither did he complain of the deterioration of Catholic family life and Catholic religious practice which are the direct results of dissent. These are serious omissions in an historic presentation by a bishop who set out to obtain wider acceptance for *Humanae Vitae*.

There is a final aspect to the Quinn talk featured on the editorial page of *Commonweal* (24 October 1980, p. 579), one which no other Catholic publication featured. Speaking of a new "World Church in the Making" the editors singled out for praise the "unprecedented consultation with the laity on the part of the Bishops' Ad Hoc Commission on Marriage and the Family (headed by Bishop Francis Stafford of Baltimore)" and "pre-synodal consultation organized by the

National Conference of both American and Canadian bishops and Notre Dame University last June 15-18." *Commonweal's* pleasure with this consultation is evidence only of what USCC's critics have been saying for years: bishops regularly consult with dissenters. Both exercises which helped fashion Quinn's thinking, to be sure, lacked participation from the nation's most famous defenders of *Humanae Vitae*.

The 1980 Bishops' Pastoral letter entitled "Catholic Higher Education and the Church's Pastoral Mission" is another example of how little effort the body of bishops expend to improve a bad situation, whenever it looks very difficult to correct. The bishops' number one problem as the Church's first teachers has to be heterodox teaching in the Catholic classroom and the inculcation of doubt or anti-magisterium attitudes there among young Catholics. In their 1980 statements condemning Marxism and capital punishment (or changing sexist language in the liturgy) the bishops took little account of the force of contrary opinions among Catholics, especially of the likely majority who possibly might favor capital punishment (or oppose changing sexist language in the liturgy). Contrariwise, for reasons of sensitivity to academic opinion, bishops demonstrated a remarkable willingness to avoid saying anything critical of what goes on in Catholic college classrooms all over the country. They avoided making any demands on the teachers responsible for the dissent which presently racks the Catholic body. What could have been one of their most important modern pastorals dealing with a major Catholic sickness came out as a tepid statement of encouragement to educators and a mere hope expressed by bishops that Catholic colleges should be good colleges and Catholic, too. Hints appear here and there in the document that problems exist, particularly when they take note of the lack of adequate Catholic formation of present day teachers in Catholic schools in comparison with earlier generations.

The strongest words in their pastoral on education were reserved for the suggestion that Catholic colleges offer students "an introduction to the Catholic theological heritage" and "a vision of life that includes religious values." This hardly states the purpose of Catholic education. The pastoral also understates the Church's difficulty with contemporary faculties when it merely expresses a hope that teachers "will have special reason to show respect for the authentic teaching of the Church." The expressed conviction of the pastoral that no conflict need exist between faculty and hierarchy did not take into account that Catholic youth in Catholic colleges are not being properly educated as Catholics or that large numbers of Catholic teachers are in open defiance of the magisterium.

Holy Ghost Father John Reedy, himself a dissenter at Notre Dame years prior to *Humanae Vitae,* read the bishops' pastoral and then congratulated their effort: "They showed restraint in avoiding a heavy-handed approach to some of the inevitable pastoral problems which arise in Catholic colleges and universities. Their statement was supportive to real problems facing these institutions, reasonably frank in pointing out some of the worries of the Catholic community" (*Long Island Catholic,* 27 November 1980). The fact that Fr. Reedy is encouraged is evidence that he and his colleagues wish episcopal support but no episcopal interference with their management of Catholic college affairs, regardless of what happens to the young.

The bishops' pastoral letter on Catholic higher education relied on the Association of American Catholic Colleges and Universities as an important resource, citing that organization's 1976 document as if the American statement had something in common with the conclusions of the Roman University Congress of 1972, which is also mentioned. Actually, ACCU's statement resists implementing the Roman statement, which was a declaration of world-wide Catholic university leaders. ACCU has recently abandoned any effort to define what a Catholic University is or ought to be and (like its parent, the NCEA College Department) the new organization is at odds with Rome on important definitions of what a Catholic college is by nature. ACCU's leading members conduct their colleges under secular rather than Catholic rules.

The bishops' 1980 pastoral letter can also be criticized for the other reasons: (1) It idealizes the current Catholic college scene which factually is a major source of Catholic defection and dissent; (2) It offers no authoritative direction from the Catholic hierarchy to university officials seeking to re-establish or maintain Catholicity; (3) It speaks of academic freedom, without providing a Catholic definition, and in spite of the great need in American Catholic higher education for responsibility to Church law and Church tradition; (4) It ignores the content of the 1972 and 1979 Roman documents on Catholic higher education, as if there was no need to re-introduce Catholic educators to their specific directives; (5) The bishops of the United States do not make any demand (as Rome does) that a college or university claiming the support of Catholics must express its institutional commitment to the Catholic faith and develop internal machinery by which that commitment can be maintained. Not only does the 1980 pastoral avoid this important requirement but it places the American bishops in the position of endorsing institutions operating according to norms unacceptable to Rome, unacceptable even to American bishops prior to 1965.

What is troublesome, too, about the bishops' statement on higher education is its selective use of Roman and papal references. For example, the 1980 pastoral singles out John Paul II's encouraging words to theologians given at the Catholic University of America (October 7, 1980), but fails to mention the context in which he uttered those words. In Section 6 of that speech the Pope bound theologians to bishops and to Catholic truth, limited their freedom by the right of the faithful to hear Catholic truth, and by the fidelity to the Church expected of theologians who profess to be Catholic.

These incidents speak for themselves. Whether the bishops responsible for their occurrence are in important or minor sees or not, there is visible a common pattern to episcopal practice in the United States for dealing with dissent: toleration of repeated violation of Vatican decrees and dissenting views in institutions directly under their jurisdiction, while standing aloof from or even restraining defenders of the magisterium.

One of the conundrums of modern episcopal leadership is the bishops' failure as chief teachers for the Church in their diocese to speak up to theologians or to confront them in face to face meetings, an opportunity which theologians use regularly to press their dissent. Yearly a local bishop is called upon to appear before the national convention of the *Catholic Theological Society of America* (CTSA) whose annual program in recent times contains a large measure of confrontation with magisterium. During the same meetings CTSA announces its theologian-of-the-year award in honor of John Courtney Murray—and, as if in defiance to Church authority, regularly bestows it on a well-known dissenter (Gerard Sloyan in 1981, David Tracy in 1980, Bernard Cooke in 1979, etc.). If the invited ordinary says anything at all he pleads more than teaches. At no time has an American bishop seized this opportunity to reiterate the criticisms of dissenting theologians made by Paul VI or John Paul II. The June 15, 1981 *NC News* reports, for example, Cincinnati's Archbishop Bernardin calling for theologians to develop "a new synthesis of Christian teaching and discipline which has been disconnected in the minds of many people"—especially in the field of Christian ethics. Having served as president of the American bishops (1974-77) Bernardin knows better than most that the hierarchy have made more accommodation with dissenters—(sometimes illicitly) than dissenters have made with bishops—if authentic teaching in local seminaries, convents, and colleges is the norm of judgment. This call on his part now for "synthesis" not compliance seems jejune and naive.

The NCCB also continues to encourage on-going debate on issues the Vatican prefers to see closed. The question is not whether discussion on certain matters is good for the Church but whether American bishops are legitimate instigators of continuing controversy about subjects which the Holy See considers to be Christian doctrine, especially with groups known to be political and contumacious opponents of the Holy See. A case in point is the debate over priestly ordination of women. The fact that NCCB meets with the *Women's Ordination Conference* (WOC) is not so significant (bishops legitimately meet with anyone), as appending its signature to a report which cites the pro-ordination position of the *Catholic Biblical Association* without citing critics of the CBA position. This is additional evidence that NCCB ("we recognize the need for further exploration") naively undercuts its own authority and that of Rome to decide doctrinal matters. It is further a matter of some surprise that bishops would enter dialogue with a WOC representative like Rosemary Reuther, an avowed revolutionary against the Church, and bring into dialogue *as agents of the NCCB* Sr. Agnes Cunningham and Sr. Mariella Frye, both of whom are public dissenters against important Catholic doctrines, over and above the priestly ordination of women! (*Origins* 25 June 1981, pp. 81 ff).

The preceding illustrations are not used to indict or denigrate particular personalities in the episcopacy or the body of bishops as a whole. However, these recitations and reminders do indicate the existence of an institutional problem of some importance. The Catholic Church no longer seems to have a policy for dealing with deviance in offices of responsibility. Not only that, dissenters have achieved enough personal security that they form a solid counter-Church in many dioceses, strong enough to neutralize the authority even of the Pope. Two questions call for firm answers: What does the Catholic Church uniquely stand for? This question deals with her basic doctrines. Secondly, how does the Church hierarchy intend to have these teachings vivify Catholic life in the coming generations? It is not possible to believe that this Church was established with two heads. Or that Peter, John, and Paul—to say nothing of Christ—would handle dissent by pretending it was a legitimate alternative to their teaching. If that had been the case, Christianity likely would not have survived to the third generation.

The Misguided Leadership
of American Bishops

4

The Body of American Bishops, not this or that bishop, has failed to
provide the governance needed for the Church during the period of
radical change following the Second Vatican Council. Had any other institution but the Catholic Church suffered similar declines and divisions, the top management personnel would by now have been re-
shuffled and the institution itself reorganized. There is a permanency of
appointment, however, for Catholic bishops sanctioned by tradition
which makes it unlikely that many of them, if any, will be fired for in-
efficiency or incompetent leadership.

An entirely different consideration also insulates bishops from
removal.

The Church is not just another corporation, nor can its effectiveness
be judged solely by statistical charts. Its spiritual dimension provides
room for suffering, often by divine intent, as an element in her recurr-
ing purification, persecution, too, as the oft-time precursor of her
restoration and renewed vitality. Only after the passage of many generations is it possible to make a judgment about what Divine Providence
might have had in mind for the Church. The sufferings of the Church
can legitimately be compared to the sufferings of Christ himself. Only
when the Resurrection occurs can the passion and death be seen in
perspective and its divine purpose understood. In a sense, therefore,
final judgments about a particular crisis in the Church are impossible
except by future historians or saints, and perhaps not even then, this
side of eternity.

However, it is commonplace to make judgments *humano modo* and
they are, of course, made regularly. Those distressed by chaos or corrup-

tion in the Church, as well as architects of ecclesiastical change who consider pain the price of new birth, make such judgments all the time. Traditionalists—if they lack a sense of the Church's human history—will never be satisfied with anything new, even if what they consider "the old Catholic standbys" are by New Testament or even by medieval standards not really old at all, certainly not instances of divine origin. On the other hand, change-making scholars and not a few willing bishops use historical precedents as excuses for their own failures, claiming among other things that since decline and dissension customarily followed every Ecumenical Council, what happened to the Church after Vatican II should be borne in patience and without complaint. One can wonder, however, why after twenty centuries of experience Church leaders have not learned to avoid the institutional mistakes of their predecessors. Church leaders are not doomed to let history take its course, as if it were a mindless force or that they were victims of historical determinism. Bishops are not compelled by the law of nature to endure suffering or to solicit disarray any more than Christ did. They surely are committed by faith to bear crosses and to ask God's help in prayer at difficult moments, even to plea for relief from Divine Punishment, if that be the explanation for the Church's plight. But *humano modo* they are expected to act with the understanding that they alone are responsible for Christ's presence in this moment of time, and, unless they believe that Christ intended to sanctify foolishness or sinfulness, to the limit of their fragile talents they must make this presence effective and meaningful. Not only are they responsible for good preaching and good works, but they are charged to root out sin, corruption, and error with a determination comparable to Christ's, when he drove money-changers from the temple.

So, while making allowance for the working of the Holy Spirit in visiting the post Vatican II Church with difficulties, judgmentalists must take account of the human evaluations Pope John Paul II is presently making. Presuming that the priest from Cracow is as much a man sent by God as any other observer, it is interesting to note that the present Pope explains the contemporary Catholic problem in human terms. He sees the source of our malaise in "a new ecclesiology strongly supported by some media of social communication," one which distorts the Second Vatican Council. And he, for one, is moving to see to it that the Catholic academic world and bishops fulfill their duty to confirm with their authority only what the teaching Church says the recent Council means (*Origins*, 28 August 1980).

But John Paul II cannot institutionalize the authentic meaning of Vatican II by himself, anymore than he can through reckless actions by the Vatican Curia. It is necessary that national conferences of Catholic bishops in each region of the Universal Church assume their share of responsibility for the pastoral care of the faithful on *authentic* terms. This is not likely to happen in the United States as long as the American bishops presume that they have done well since 1965, or as long as they fail to recognize the extent to which they have contributed to the problems they now face.

The following overview of their conduct in the post-conciliar years, which is offered as helpful diagnosis, leads this writer to conclude that bishops have made *three* substantial errors of judgment which must be corrected if true reform on the authentic lines of Vatican II is to proceed apace, and if the pontificate of John Paul II is to do what Paul VI could hardly persuade or coerce anyone to do—conform to Catholic law.

1 . *Bishops misread the intentions of dissenters and the extent to which their influence contributed to the decline of Catholic institutions.*
2. *The Bishops' strategy of diffusing dissent through dialogue with their antagonists, while keeping supporters of the magisterium at a distance, has had the effect of institutionalizing dissent in Church structures and enhancing its respectability.*
3. *Bishops have failed to be the hierarchy of the Catholic Church.*

The *first two failures* have been amply illustrated throughout this analysis. Of the two the first error is more excusable. The early post-conciliar era was a period of experimentation which called for latitude at lower levels of the Church, wider than anything known in the preceding century. *Furthermore,* most of the bishops had been chosen by Rome to lead and manage a settled and highly successful church. Their talents were commensurate with the Church's needs of that time. Since no one in 1962 could have anticipated ecclesiastical turmoil, it would be unfair to blame men chosen to supervise a peaceful church for their inability to manage a stormy church. However, the signs of the bad intentions and revolutionary goals of dissenters became obvious very early, making the second error less understandable. The revolt of Catholic university presidents led by Robert Henle, SJ, and Theodore Hesburgh, CSC, began in 1967 with "Land O'Lakes". The revolt of Catholic theologians began with Charles Curran in 1967 and continued with him, Walter Burghardt, SJ, and Richard McCormick, SJ in 1968 and to this day. By 1970 Sr. Mary Elise, SND, executive director of the *Consortium Perfectae Caritatis,* was able to report on a meeting held in April of that year in Chicago during which thirty superiors of religious orders of men and thirty others for women composed what effectively can be called the new agenda for the second level managers of the Church's patrimony in education and welfare. This agenda specified that Rome's directives on religious life be ignored, that the vows of poverty and obedience be stripped of any sensible meaning. Flight from convents and monasteries laid the groundwork for married religious. Within a half decade bishops were embroiled in a religious education crisis, a severe drop in Mass attendance and religious vocations, and empty confessional lines. By 1971 the bishops were being told by theologians hired to do research on their behalf, that bishops are not really successors of the apostles and that there were no such thing as priests in the primitive Church.

Normally all these onslaughts on institutional integrity and identity would call for defensive countermeasures.

When a breakdown becomes apparent or the siege on institutional strongholds become ominous the normal thing for leaders to do, especially if they are unprepared, is to retrench as necessary, while they regroup their best resources for defense or counterattack. Corporation presidents and labor leaders do this; government officials do it, generals do it. The American bishops chose another course. Almost immediately they negotiated with their antagonists. Agreements — such as those in higher education — resulted in the complete takeover of major Catholic institutions by dissenters. Hand in hand with appeasement of enemies went (with bishops' passive concurrence at least) the isolation of defenders of the magisterium, the bishops' normal allies in exercising the teaching office. It seems incongruous now that in 1963, when the Catholic doctrine on contraception was universally accepted within the American Catholic academic world, the bishops made no effort to organize the vast majority of the American theologians (including Charles Curran and Richard McCormick) in support of Church doctrine. They were teaching then that contraception was intrinsically evil. Instead, they permitted important officials inside National Catholic Welfare Conference (predecessor to USCC) to promote contraception and the new theology, allowed Hans Kung and Bernard Haring to move around the country unchallenged, re-educating their religious and their teachers in dissent. They did little to prevent the secularization of their colleges and religious communities, standing aside while the giants of that period's theology —- John Ford, John Lynch, and Joseph Farraher — were sent into exile and the parish priests' manual *Theological Studies* fell into the hands of dissenters.

This appeasement by bishops continues to the present day. It took ten years for the NCCB to recognize that Catholic institutions were in shambles because of theological dissent. Many theologians, far from enriching or supporting the teaching of the Church, had already declared their independence of that teaching as expounded by the magisterium, making of themselves a magisterium in their own right.

Among the prominent names associated with theological deviance were Raymond Brown, Avery Dulles, Richard McCormick, Charles Curran, and men associated with them such as Fredrick McManus; later student practitioners of the new theology were Timothy O'Connell, Joseph Komanchak, and Agnes Cunningham. The NCCB decided it must do something to alleviate this condition in May 1976. It established a Committee on Doctrine, the purpose of which was the better exposition and defense of the teaching of the magisterium. Almost immediately, however, the NCCB Committee fell into the hands of Catholic University of American professors where dissent was centralized. Instead of dealing with the teaching of authentic Catholic doctrine, the participating bishops followed an agenda determined by Catholic University of America professors. Academic participation was restricted to the theologians who were the source of the very doctrinal problems the bishops were trying to correct. Bishops listened to papers on why the present Church model was wrong, why bishops should lead Rome, not follow, why bishops should follow the dissenting theologians instead. The 1977 Report of the Bishops' Committee on Doctrine is devoted to citing the opinions of Avery Dulles, Timothy O'Connell, *Commonweal,* Richard McCormick, and Sr. Agnes Cunningham. At one point in the report the suggestion is made that a bishop might better be called the "ordinary spokesman for Church teaching", rather than teacher, reducing him to a public relations role, hardly the position contemplated by *Lumen Gentium.* The 1980 report shows that three years of dialogue has not advanced bishops toward the accomplishment of their doctrinal purposes. Contrariwise, the *Origins* account of their meetings (7 February 1980) makes it clear that the bishops have persuaded these theologians of very little. The participating theologians, on the other hand, continue in these meetings to insist on their own alternatives to the teachings of Vatican II. They may not have succeeded in changing the structures of the Church (or its doctrines), but their status as consultors to bishops makes their classroom advocacy of dissent more credible and more influential. The erosion of the influence of the magisterium in Catholic colleges, seminaries, monasteries and convents continues.

From an institutional viewpoint the NCCB Committee's operational procedures are ill-conceived. It is a mistake (and self-destructive if done with forethought) for the Body of Bishops to consult nationally on a regular basis with certain priests who are never consulted by their own local ordinaries. But the vital interest of the Church is more certainly endangered, once dialogue becomes an habitual rule, if theological dissenters participate in these meetings more often than defenders of the magisterium. Why should bishops listen to Avery

Dulles, SJ, without also listening to John Sheets, SJ, (Creighton) or Earl Weis, SJ, (Loyola) or Donald Keefe, SJ (Loyola)? When Richard McCormick, SJ, is making his exceptions to Catholic moral prescriptions, why are bishops (not the pope) not discovering how wrong he is—from William May (CUA) or William Smith (Dunwoodie) or Germain Grisez (Mount St. Mary's) or Joseph Farraher, SJ (San Francisco). The list of the magisterium's scholarly defenders is long but few have a prominent place in the bishops' consultative process.

This observation leads to the *third* and most troublesome aspect of post-Vatican II Catholicism, viz. the decline of hierarchy itself. "Hierarchy" means "holy rule", "sacred rule", "priestly rule". Catholic doctrine says that hierarchy—bishops with pope—are the chief witnesses and guarantors of Christ's revelation. This is a role they can share but cannot abandon—any more than Christ did or would. In a legitimate sense Christ was hierarchy personified. He was the Message from the Father. His message was not one deduced from the folklore and experience of the Jewish people. As Christ fulfilled, interpreted, and sanctioned God's first revelation through Jewish patriarchs, prophets, judges, and kings, so Catholic bishops proclaim and authenticate Christ's *evangelium*.

Episcopal statements still proclaim the authoritative status of the episcopate but American bishops appear more as brothers to their people than fathers, more as facilitators obtaining agreement about what Christ really intended than as bold preachers of the revealed word, more as one branch of Church government than as bishops acting in Christ's name. There are human reasons for their new look. Some of their predecessors were at times high-handed managers of the local Church—monarchs (in its pejorative sense) rather than hierarchs. Modern bishops, wishing to counter an autocratic impression, have opted for the companionate image. Then too, as conservative types, they could have been expected to cede some status when required to give up their thrones and ermine capes. A third explanation for their new image may be found in a Vatican II decision to bring priests, religious, laity into the governance of the Church. Shared authority sometimes has been followed by abdicated authority. Rarely in recent years have bishops exercised episcopal authority (defined in Church law) unless the subject of the enforcement was a willing subject. Penalties for law breaking are less common in today's Church than in the secular state, which is plagued by intolerable crime and social deviance of epidemic proportions. The normal principle of good order in the Church (which has few extraordinary worldly rewards or punishments to motivate compliance) is the virtue or vow of obedience. In the contemporary Church, however, a religious is "ordered" under obedience to do what he wants or what he already has consented to do. The hierarchical structure of the Church has been compromised at all levels. Pastors and religious superiors—once solely responsible for the implementation of Church policies, are now virtual figureheads. Unsurprisingly, therefore, the offices have become attractive only to those who wish to change Church policies or to challenge Catholic doctrine.

The human reasons so far mentioned, however, are still not the real reasons for the decline of Church hierarchy. Bishops' toleration of disobedience by priests and religious teachers is the main cause. A teacher in the Church normally is another Catholic, no more nor less. He is bound by Church law, and by Church definitions like all Catholics. The reason for this kind of ecclesiastical egalitarianism is the fact that—in a way unknown to secular society—the religious truth Catholics profess is determined by authority—Christ first, the Church later. The casuist makes many distinctions about what faith requires under obedience, but if he makes too many distinctions one is entitled to ask whether he believes Church authority can define religious truth at all. If the Church cannot define with security what the content of Christ's revelation really is, there is no objective basis to the faith of the believer. If academicians reject this norm of belief, all Catholics are free to deny it. Once Charles Curran and Richard J. McCormick dethrone the pope, they make everyman his or her own pope. If we do not need a pope, nor need to follow him, we certainly have no need of a Curran or McCormick. Our conscience settles whatever faith we have, if we need have any at all.

Catholic theologians have in recent years even gone beyond disobedience. Their rationale for disobedience raises serious doubts about the believability of Christianity itself. The uncertainties created by academicians become an acute problem for bishops. Toleration of disobedience may at times indicate episcopal weakness or poor leadership. But bishops' appearance to acquiesce in the dissenters' rationale strikes at the credibility of the Catholic faith itself.

The rationale for dissent—designed to appeal to nonbelievers or half-believers who find Christianity's supernatural claims unscientific—is based upon alleged research discoveries of recent scholarship. One or another theologian can be found to assert one or the other of the following propositions:

- No such thing as "revelation" exists if this mean "God-out-there" once upon a time sent men to speak for Him to other men.
- The Bible, no longer accepted as revelation in this sense, represents instead the religious experience of a people searching for the one God

they believe made Heaven and Earth.

- In this latter sense Scripture can be called "revelation"—i.e. the written record of "God"—the original cosmic force—working out in an evolutionary way nature's original endowment.
- The Jews prophesied nothing, not even about a Messiah. Because they were always a persecuted people they verbalized instead over many centuries their longing for a redeemer.
- Jesus was a teacher (rabbi) in the Jewish tradition, a tradition he accepted, one in which he played a reformer's role.
- During his lifetime Jesus remained a 1st Century Jew with the personal limitations and superstitions of his background.
- There is serious question whether Jesus ever considered himself "Son of God", except in the customary Jewish sense.
- How much Jesus knew of his "divine sonship" is also a matter of some dispute.
- Jesus' knowledge of future events was inaccurate.
- His so-called prophesies and miracles are not necessarily disruptions of natural processes, but glowing accounts of his sayings and doings written under the influence of post-Resurrection enthusiasm by people who never saw him first hand.
- What the resurrection really meant is hard to say (it probably did not mean "physical resuscitation" but his followers did believe in his return from the dead and in his post-crucifixion "appearances".
- It was the disciples who created the separate Christian church after they were exiled by the synagogue establishment.
- Christ intended to reform Judaism, not begin a new religion.
- We cannot be certain how many New Testament statements were Christ's actual words, not even the texts customarily used to "prove" the foundation of the Church, the primacy of Peter, apostolic succession of bishops, the institution of the Mass as a Sacrifice, the Priesthood and the Sacraments.
- Christ never defined dogmas or prescribed moral codes, except to tell his followers to love God, to love and take care of each other.
- The early Church was a community of followers more than a corporate body instituted by him.
- The primitive church took on many forms of government and adopted different, often contradictory, doctrines. Under the force of God's spirit that church developed in divergent ways, some of which are distortions of or unnecessary accretions to the original Christian gospel.

Different dissenting scholars raise different doubts or draw the line between belief and unbelief at different points. Only the most radical theologians subscribe to all the above propositions. But there is far more agreement on most of them—at least on the doubts—than bishops are inclined to appreciate. There is an even larger amount of agreement among dissenters on at least two propositions: (1) As a result of scholarly research the right of the hierarchy to bind consciences on most particularities of faith and morals must be denied or at least cast into serious doubt; (2) In the practical order the effective way to limit the hierarchy's rights over moral teaching is to redefine the church in terms of the "People of God" and to consider their religious experience as a better modern guide to "revelation" than ancient documents, no matter how venerable or "sacred". Donald Thorman, editor of the *National Catholic Reporter* (11 December 1970), expressed gratitude to the reformers for ending the right of "churchmen in high places to determine the conduct of their private lives." Richard McBrien takes the other route. He predicts that during the 1980's the laity will turn the institutional Church with its emphasis on hierarchy to the "Church as People" who will assume policy-making power over Church business. Whether one follows Thorman or McBrien, the contemplated Church is not likely to be Catholic, especially if the McBriens can give their dissident views directly to religious education congresses, sponsored by bishops, as he did in Milwaukee (*The Milwaukee Journal,* 16 August 1980).

The problems of the American Church, then, are not minor. If John Paul II's doctrinal pronouncements and disciplinary decisions are normative for bishops, there are serious divergencies between the Pope and the *practice* of the American bishops. The divergencies in principle are not major at this point. During his visit (October 1979) to the American bishops in Chicago, the pope, in order to highlight the Church's contemporary problem, drew on that hierarchy's own repeated pronouncements. He was aware that long before his arrival in Rome Vatican authorities spoke privately of "the emerging American Church" as if a new form of Gallicanism was in the offing. John Paul II does not mind Americanism as long as it is Catholic, and as long as the American Catholic performance is up to its traditional standards. Hence his use of American magisterial statements to reinforce his own judgment about the future policies of the Church.

But, says the pope, little constructive can be accomplished unless dissent is first delimited and religious discipline is restored. As of this moment, however, the American bishops have not developed a concrete program to deal with the deeply imbedded heterodoxy of their own institutions, a heterodoxy sometimes encouraged by particular bishops. The dissenters have discovered the contemporary bishops' weak spot. The last complaint a bishop today wishes to receive is one about heterodoxy or false teaching. In the face of a complaint, he either contends that the complaints are illegitimate (which they sometimes are), that the complainers are pathological personalities (as they sometimes are), that the charges are false or that the Church recognizes theological pluralism (all of which may sometimes be true), or that some other bishop has jurisdiction. In their turn bishops are not obtuse. They know that lecturers and teachers within their jurisdictions, sometimes in their seminaries, are suborning Catholic doctrine. But like the Dutch bishops, they are afraid of the media and avoid involving themselves in any theological controversy which looks newsworthy. Sometimes they issue bland statements of protest against particular offenses which everyone knows are not intended for implementation. There is not record of an American bishop mounting his *cathedra* to denounce specific error, except the well-reported cases of Cardinal McIntyre (Fr. William Dubay), Cardinal O'Boyle (more than 19 priests), lately Bishop Joseph V. Sullivan of Baton Rouge, who were all scorned for their actions. Sometimes a bishop invites a dissenter to give lectures or Lenten sermons in his Cathedral, perhaps with the hope that episcopal benevolence will be reciprocated, which it usually is not.

Bishops increasingly appear as tolerators of or collaborators in dissent. One situation is no less dangerous to the Church than the other. In such cases the involved bishops or body of bishops, whether they realize it or not, become symbols of an evolving Church turning its back on its own definitions, of a new church in the making after the model proposed by dissenters. In these circumstances orthodox bishops, orthodox scholars and faithful who commit themselves to the Church's creeds, appear as remnants of the Church simplistic, Catholics totally irrelevant to the modern thrust of the new Church. The fact that the body of bishops ignore orthodox scholars is only one bad sign. Their frequent cohabitation with dissenters is another. An inexcusable situation arises when bishops appear to be harassing defenders of the magisterium (for all their faults) or appear unfriendly to dissenters' critics (for all their faults). One begins to wonder on whose side the bishops actually are. Or whom they wish to have on their side. Or whether their unity with John Paul II is real or illusory.

Where Do the Bishops Go from Here?

5

This is a critical question: If collegiality is a two way street, they go with the pope. But this means that the abusers of Vatican II and the false teachers in its name must sooner or later be confronted by the bishops. The hierarchy which wrote Vatican II's documents and hopefully knows what it intended cannot afford to let the Council's pronouncements become dead letters. On the other hand, because almost twenty years of vacillating have gone by, the bishops will have no easy task. Catholics will need reeducation. Many have been led to believe that almost anything can now be permitted to them without disturbing their conscience, church membership or salvation. The bishops' most difficult assignment, of course, will be the elimination from Catholic institutions of those who no longer believe in the Church's essential truths even though they still use traditional Catholic language. The American hierarchy must face up to the dark fact that the new Christianity now nurturing in the Church's womb—the new world religion, if you will—has a new god (the World) and a new high priest (Humanity). Unless checked soon, the optimum future bishops can expect is to preside over a worldwide Anglican-type Catholicism—high, middle, low churches to suit all tastes, not exactly the Church contemplated by the Council Fathers 1962-1965. If these directions are not Catholic, and they surely are not, what specifically must bishops do to reverse the alien drift of Catholicism?

Bishops must become preachers of the Word
American bishops of the 19th century used their pulpits and lecture halls to good advantage. Faced with hostility from believing Protestants they regularly preached on theological or ascetical subjects. St. John

Neumann was a preacher. Bishop John Hughes often lectured and ser-
monized on the divinity of Christ, Mary's Immaculate Conception, the
infallibility of the Pope. The Baltimore Councils were preaching synods
and their documents, including the *Baltimore Catechism*, were
evangelical in nature. Cardinal Gibbons' *Faith of Our Fathers*, written
in 1876, was a fantastically successful *vade mecum* for preachers well into
the twentieth century. Later, Archbishops like Glennon, Hanna and
Schrembs were looked upon as prominent preachers. As the bishops
preached so did pastors. Secular newspapers freely quoted the outstanding preachers of those days. In a word, the bishops of the emerging
Church of the United States, and the pastors they moulded, were not
afraid to be apologists for the unique and supernatural claims of the
Church. There is no reason why today's bishops need be less courageous,
even though their contemporary antagonists are secularized Catholics,
not Protestants. In modern times Fulton Sheen was a unique bishop.

The present Pope gives a good example of what a modern bishop
must be. He calls himself Peter the Apostle, but he is also Paul, mis-
sioner to unbelievers and half-believers. John Paul II's preaching and
praying priorities are the first and essential requirements of the
bishops' ministry. However, if bishops are to imitate the pope, they
must be secure in the knowledge of what they preach and in what
order they preach the Church's truth. A Catholic hierarchy of values
suggests that they moralize. John Paul went out of his way at Trinity
College in Washington, D.C. (October 7, 1979) to tell an ecumenical
audience that moral life depends on the life of faith, that "deep divisions" between churches over moral matters reflect divergencies in
faith. The life of faith calls for special exposition today, because it is
the life of faith which is being drained from the Church Body. In the
absence of authentic faith, a bishop can expect little hearing for his
moral directives, unless, of course, he conspires to encourage his people to continue a life of sin. But because today's Catholics are better
educated than their forbearers, the bishop must now preach with
theological competence and conviction. If his own theology is
distorted or if he mutes the doctrines difficult for secularized Christians to believe, the last state of the faithful may be worse than the
first.

Inevitably, of course, the bishop must address himself to the quality
of moral life demanded by commitment to the Catholic faith. A
bishop's concern for weak sinners in the Church must always be
sincere, but he must be mindful, too, of the "hypocrites" and the
"whitened sepulchers" within the Church. At times he must tell his
flock what they do not want to hear—that they are sinners. In our
moral climate they will often resent the bishop's preaching the need of

redemption—(a role their parents considered legitimate) precisely because they think much like their secular peers. However, if past experience is any norm, those who truly believe will be grateful in the end.

When the bishop attends to questions of morality, he must speak of the upright life and personal sins before he pronounces on social ills. This is the Christian priority. Pius XI in *Quadragesimo Anno* called the reform of morals as the "first and most necessary" remedy for social disorder. Secular man does not place great value on personal goodness, as long as social life is good, i.e. prosperous, peaceful, free. The Catholic bishop accepts the importance of good institutions and realizes that bad institutions inhibit moral virtue. Nonetheless, the bishop is leading men, not institutions, to salvation. He must speak first of natural and supernatural virtues, the Beatitudes, the Counsels of Perfection, the Ten Commandments, the Precepts of the Church— directives which were given to human persons. If bishops in former days fell short of their own expectations by failure to speak more often of sins committed by social groups, the temptation today is in the opposite direction—i.e. a neglect to lead people to an examination of conscience for personal sin with a view toward bringing them to contrition and firm purpose of amendment.

As for social morality, bishops should form consciences of the faithful here with similar intelligence and courage. But they must speak as priests and theologians, not as social scientists or political experts. Pope John Paul II is a master of articulating the Church's social gospel, even as he eschews taking the place of lay experts and civil leaders in developing the practical programs. Some Catholics take for granted that bishops or the pope must talk to sins associated with the Ten Commandments, forgetting that the commandments bind the conduct of institutional leaders as well as private persons. The bishop cannot avoid the social issues involved in the violation of human rights, war, poverty, etc. The law that guides the Christian conscience on adultery and abortion should guide the conscience of those in a position to alleviate social conditions which de-moralize individual consciences or adversely affect the practice of virtue. Unlike politicians who expect support of social causes to mean votes on election day, bishops rarely gain church-goers through social preachments. Indeed, they may lose some. The bishops' motive in preaching the moral law can only be the claim of God's word and their responsibility to preach it.

There are traps, however, lurking for bishops moralizing about social conditions that are not present when they speak of personal morality. Stealing ten dollars from the grocery owner's till is much easier to adjudicate as a moral case than the possible theft of thousands of dollars in a sharp business deal by an executive of a supermarket chain. Buying a gun for personal self-defense and buying thousands of nuclear warheads are subject to moral evaluation based on the same principles, but determination of morality and immorality in the second situation is a more complicated process. Paul VI admitted in *Octagesima Adveniens* (1971) that complex social situations make it "difficult to utter a unified message and to put forward a solution which has universal validity." Cardinal Krol, speaking for the hierarchy on the nuclear arms race, also acknowledged that on subjects like this, the bishops agree only on general principles. Even when the NCCB chooses to make a prudential judgment, as it did in approving the Salt II agreement (*America,* 8 March 1980, pp. 183-185), such recommendations are NCCB's judgments, which do not bind the consciences of Catholics.

There is still another trap for bishops who moralize on social situations. When dissenting theologians note how bishops depend on political experience in making these judgments and the tentativeness of their recommendation in such matters, they develop the argument that episcopal judgments on marriage and sexuality are equally tentative, and must be measured equally by the human experience of married couples. Charles Curran, for example, would deny bishops the last word on Salt II, but the last word on adultery also, unless they had the concurrence of adulterers (*America,* 1 March 1980, p. 166).

However, in extraordinary cases the bishops can bind Catholic consciences on matters of social morality—in clear cases of bigotry by Catholics or the denial of basic human rights by employers or government, certainly on issues like direct abortion. In the United States bishops ordinarily do not think in these terms, and in most cases their restraint reflects the complexity of the issues and the political climate of the country, where the use of such ecclesiastical authority would be counter-productive. However, Pope Pius XII during the 1948 Italian elections did not hesitate to impose a moral obligation on Catholics to reject Communist officeholders. The issue then was the proximate danger of a Communist take-over of a poverty stricken post-war Italy and the well-being of the Church under such a regime.

In summary, therefore, the bishops must be careful on social pronouncements but not bland. Once certain of their issue—the good of moral life, the family, civil order, the Church—they must be forthright defenders and preachers of the Word, at some cost to themselves, if need be. During the present internal crisis of the church they must be prepared to contest *nominatim* if necessary those who defy the magisterium or misuse the priestly or religious office. The alternative

is capitulation to worldly standards and the degradation of the
episcopal office.

*Bishops must insist that theological investigations and presentations
take place in conformity with Catholic norms.*

Thus far the bishops have permitted without protest the new
theologians to write and act if secular norms govern the Catholic
theological enterprise. The Lindbeck Report (1976) drafted for the
Rockefeller Foundation established that the modern theological enterprise, whether Catholic or Protestant, tends to be less theological (i.e.
less doctrinal) and more non-sectarian than heretofore. The Catholic
theologians with whom bishops frequently engage in dialogue ex-
emplify how much a part of this trend they have become. These
theologians approach their research and teaching as if in complete
detachment from their commitment to the Church or to the
magisterium. One evidence of this development is Richard McBrien's
new and highly praised two volume work entitled *Catholicism,* which
discusses the Church's doctrine (even rejecting some of it) as if a reader
may freely choose between the teaching of the magisterium or that of
dissenting theologians. An authentic Catholic theologian, however,
begins and ends both research and teaching in full and obvious commitment to the magisterium. This is an essential part of his
methodology.

The *International Theological Commission* (ITHC) through five annual meetings (1970-1975) explored the relationship of the
magisterium and Catholic theology. These sessions were held in full
awareness that theologians after the Council (led first by dissenters in
Europe) became a class-conscious interest group tending to consider
themselves autonomous of Church authority. They have not only ex-
aggerated their autonomy since then, but have mistakenly identified
theology as simply another independent science, whereas in truth, if it
is Catholic, it is the Church's science. The ITHC deliberations resulted
in the publication of twelve theses which situate Catholic theologians
"in medio ecclesiae" and subject them to the magisterium (*La
Documentation Catholique* 18 July 1976). The key elements in the
ITHC report affecting controversial theologians seem to be the following:

1 . Theologians have a pastoral and missionary responsibility in the
    Church. They must not only intend this but they must be pastoral
    and missionary in fact. (Theses 3)

    In effect, their teaching and writing must show reverence to the
    faithful's spiritual interest and the Church's chief pastors.

2. The authentic interpretation of the Word of God and the condem-
    nation of errors belongs to the magisterium, not to theologians.

Theologians "lend their aid to the task of spreading, clarifying, confirming and defending the truth which magisterium authoritatively propounds." (Theses 5)

The theologian's task is to help implant the Church's doctrine in the thinking of contemporary man, not to uproot it.

3. The Catholic theologian is not engaged in a profane enterprise. He is exercising a "genuinely ecclesial authority", which he usually derives from his canonical mission. He is sent to preach and teach by pope and bishops in a way no different than the apostles who were sent by Christ. Even if this canonical mission has not been explicated, theologizing can only be done in communion with the faith, and this means with the magisterium. (Thesis 7)

In effect, this requires that the Catholic theologian, once he leaves his library to spread his learning in the public forum, needs the authorization of the magisterium.

4. There are limits to a Catholic theologian's freedom. Not only is he bound by the truth, but by his responsibility to the Church. Even when exercising a critical function with his theologizing, he must do this positively, not destructively, i.e. he must never impair the content or meaning of revelation. (Thesis 8)

5. Magisterium and theologians must be in habitual association by virtue of their common sharing of one faith. This means ongoing dialogue and mutual exchange. Bishops and theologians, however, are not peers. At the end of dialogue theologians are accountable to bishops. And there are limits to dialogue. Dialogue ceases "when the limits of faith are reached." Dialogue ceases also when it becomes a political tool or an instrument for publicizing issues in dispute or to bring pressure on Church authority from without. Nor does dialogue mean that something is "uncertain and utterly unknown". Dialogue more often concerns a truth which "has been revealed and handed on to the Church to be faithfully kept." (Theses 10-11)

6. If competent authority cannot persuade a theologian by informal and largely private means, then an "official examination of a theologian's writings" can follow. Disciplinary measures from "verbal sanctions" to charges of heresy can then be employed.

In other words, theologians cannot contest the magisterium unendingly without expecting effective response from Church authority in defense of the faith. ITHC member Karl Lehmann concludes his analysis of the twelve theses with this reminder: "[Thesis 12] clearly recognizes that dialogue comes to an end when the theologian definitely contradicts the truth of faith. In this case, it is the theologian himself who in the last analysis has refused the dialogue." (USCC 1977 Translation of the Twelve Theses, p. 18.)

Even though the twelve theses are delicately phrased there is no question that ITHC—a commission composed of such theologians as Barnabas Ahern, CP, Fr. Yves Congar, Mgr. Phillippe Delhaye—reiterated standard Catholic norms for the theological enterprise which have not governed the conduct of American theologians since 1965. Dissenters are not known for confirming or defending the truth proclaimed by the magisterium. Instead, they consider their pastoral responsibility to include freeing the faithful from the restraints imposed by the magisterium, do not recognize themselves as subject to Church authority, reject the idea of canonical mission, demand that their freedom extend as far as American civil law will protect it, use threats and publicity to cow bishops, admit no limits in practice to dialogue, act as if all truths they declare controversial to be uncertain, if not unknown. They refuse at times to appear before competent authority, save on terms common to secular legal processes, and are more likely to sanction Church authority than be sanctioned by it.

It is little wonder that American theologians resent the Holy See, which judges their works by Catholic norms exclusively. Nor is it surprising that the Catholic Theological Society of America prefers that judgment, if it need be made at all, be made by a local American bishop, not Rome. By entering dialogue as the peers of theologians or as if theologians were equal partners in propounding the faith, bishops have compromised their role in the Church. They come to this kind of dialogue as if they were students, not as competent teachers in their own right. Bishops are not theologians' peers, but judges of and decision-makers on theological matters whenever and however Catholic doctrine is involved.

Contemporary bishops make another mistake, one not made by their predecessors a generation removed. By mainly engaging in dialogue with dissenters, they remain underinfluenced by the scholars who satisfy Catholic and scientific standards. They also become intimidated by what they come to look upon as an irresistible force. Some bishops leave meetings—at Notre Dame, for example—awed by the depth and obstinacy of dissent and afraid more than ever to stand up to it. Like Abraham of old they could find themselves standing before the Lord unable to find fifty or forty or twenty, maybe not even ten first-rate moral theologians teaching in major seminaries or universities in conformity with their official teaching.

The differing approach to dialogue taken by American bishops and theologians is startling. Charles Curran and Archbishop John Whealon participated in a Detroit forum where these styles appeared in sharp contrast. Curran simply and categorically denied that moral life is centrally related to faith and reasserted his right (and anyone else's) to publicly dissent from Church teaching. What should bishops do when faced by confrontation, asks Curran: "Bishops should encourage theologians but not necessarily adopt whatever they say" (*National Catholic Reporter*, 4 July 1980, p. 8). Such a cosy position guarnatees that Curran is looking to remain untouched by bishops either in their teaching or by their authority. He brings bishops down to his level. He makes the bishop's doctrinal statement merely another man's opinion, no better nor worse than his own. It follows, therefore, that when NCCB bans contraceptive sterilization in Catholic hospitals, it becomes perfectly proper for a theologian (Richard McCormick) to contradict it: "It's not always morally wrong" (*National Catholic Reporter* 18 July 1980).

How does an experienced dialoguer like Archbishop Whelan deal with such confrontation? He does not confront because he wishes to be agreeable. He certainly does not deal with the Currans and McCormicks as they deal with bishops. Nor does he assert that a Christian's moral code proceeds directly from the quality of his faith, that dissenters are in disobedience, that they are subject to strictures once reserved by Christ for those who scandalize members of the flock.

Hartford's archbishop attempted in a Washington colloquium to ingratiate himself at the outset with his unfriendly audience. He did this by apologizing for the Church's "conservatives". Whelan describes these as sour types, fundamentalists, Latin Mass extremists, members of the John Birch Society, disoriented and insecure psychological types. He had problems, too, with "progressives" but they were of a different genre. Progressives' problems, says Whelan, are not psychological (e.g. adolescent confrontations with authority), but epistemological. They tend to look upon reality dynamically, not statically like conservatives. The course for bishops is to stand aloof above these polarized types, father to all, alienating no one. A strong stand by the bishop for either side of the ideological spectrum may cause serious harm to the Church. The Hartford Archbishop ends up agreeing with the Charles Currans, even concluding that the pluralism dissenting theologians speak about is normal in the church (*Catholic Mind*, July 1980).

As long as the theological enterprise is conducted on these terms— as long as bishops contribute to the impression that the polarization in the Church results merely from the collision of theological approaches, not from rejection of doctrine, John Paul II will find himself fighting his battle for the faith alone. At least he will be fighting without any vigorous support from American bishops.

The Bishops must duly implement the Holy See's decrees and the

General Law of the Church.

They do not do this with consistency. A case can be made that American lawlessness has overwhelmed the Church whose one-time stability was admired by many Americans. The present breakdown in Church unity is due in part to the toleration by bishops of flagrant religious crimes.

Good Catholic order does not mean tyranny, because the Church is designed to be a home, not a jail. For this reason bishops during their lifetime are called upon to be fathers, not martinets, good pastors, not hirelings. They will perforce observe a good deal of wandering by members of the flock during their journey. But whether the image of father or pastor is used to describe the bishop's role, it is toward virtue, not vice, towards obeying law, not taking law into their own hands, to being better than the law demands, not satisfied even with venial sin, that he moves.

Prior to Vatican II Catholic deviance co-existed with order. Bad social conduct was neither condoned nor tolerated, especially if grave scandal or public nuisance was an issue. Priests and religious were expected to be particularly law-abiding. Catholic tranquility did not come about overnight. It was unruly priests and impious laity which prompted responsible pastors to ask Rome in 1789 for the first American bishop. John Carroll's consecration only marked the beginning of a century-long struggle to turn rowdy immigrants into practicing Catholics and socially acceptable Americans. That process of religious formation has now been reversed by dissidents. Even books written to hail a new Church aborning — Andrew Greeley's, Eugene Kennedy's, Gregory Baum's, Peter Hebblethwaite's — testify to massive disobedience, incited often by those who ask for Vatican II constitutions to become the law of the Church. They sometimes hail those bishops who rebel against the strictures contained in those decrees.

The curious aspect of this is that the renewal of Catholicism — promised by Vatican II — depends on the execution of laws and regulations issued by Rome and bishops to implement the Council. Hundreds of minor directives have been issued since 1965 as part of the renewal process. Major pronouncements have also been made by pope and sacred congregations about new procedures for liturgical celebrations, diocesan management, priestly and religious life, ecumenism, catechetics and Catholic universities. Those promulgated by Paul VI on liturgy (1964), on bishops (1965), on religious life (1971), John Paul II's *Catechesi Tradendae* and *Sapientia Christiana* (1979) on education (which were really Paul's) are historic in their Catholic content.

Aggiornomento for the Catholic Church is impossible without laws reasonably enforced and reasonably observed. These laws will be observed to the extent they are enforced. Enforcement involves imposing penalties on violators. Archbishop Lefebvre, for example, goes about his business because he thinks the Church is not serious about his particular violations. If the Church is really serious about his aberrations, he (according to him) has not been punished enough. Lefebvre proves the adage that good people are those who want to be good, but also those who keep an eye on the police.

The Church's public law is, therefore, the instrument through which the hierarchy will work out the objectives of Vatican II. Not only will that law condition the behavior of the believers, regardless of their private preferences, but it normally controls outrageous conduct which jeopardizes the goals of Vatican II and the Church. Most people favor law — because they recognize that in its absence the law-abiding become the victims of deviants. Law-breakers have been with the Church from the early days of the magicians Simon and Elymas and the thief Ananias. The new problem is the dissent and disobedience of religious employed in Church positions of trust, abetted by bishops ignoring or disobeying the pope in ways which would not be tolerated by the first Peter, the first John, or the first Paul.

Under the cover of authorized change, flagrant violations of the Church's general law have gone unpunished. The excuse usually has been that the Code of Canon Law, adopted in 1918, was itself outmoded. However, though new legislation annulled, amended or superseded significant Sections of "the Code", as it is commonly called, most of the 2414 canons in that code still govern Catholic conduct, especially the general rules concerning a priest's responsibilities, the teaching authority of the Church, and offenses against the Church.

Consider the canons at the very end of the Code dealing with abuse or misuse of the Eucharist (Cn. 2320), the usurpation of the priestly office (Cn. 2320), disobedience of pope or bishops (Cn. 2331), recourse to secular power to impede the hierarchy's rule of authority over the Church (Cn. 2333), priests inciting laity to interfere with Church authority or preventing pastors from being named or removed (Cn. 2337), participation in abortion (Cn. 2350), apostasy or flight from religious life (Cn. 2385) attempted civil marriages by priests (Cn. 2388). The penalties for offenses of these kinds range from warnings to suspensions and excommunications. Some penalties were automatic, as for the woman or doctor involved in abortion or for priests attempting a civil marriage.

Violations of these canons (which are still Church law) are now commonplace without any noticeable effort by bishops to impose or announce the penalties. Depositing particles of hosts in garbage cans or the conducting of sacred liturgy on a city's main street to publicize a social protest, court cases brought or threatened against bishops who seek to enforce Catholic law on disobedient priests or professors, alienation of Church property by disaffected religious—without contestation by bishops—has helped bring all Catholic law into disrepute. This has been a source of scandal to an older generation trained to respect Church law, and bad example to Catholic youth whose disregard, if not contempt, for Catholic law is well known.

What to do about this disarray? Nothing at all, of course, if the decisions and the teachings of the magisterium are no longer normative. Those who sincerely believe that we are in transit to the Church of Vatican III (ostensibly a pluralistic ecumenical body), in the supremacy of conscience over the magisterium as a moral norm, or in the right of veto inherent in a democratic church are willing to accept disarray. This is the pluralism of which they speak, although in practice they themselves enforce their own orthodoxy whenever they are in power. Corrective action and the enforcement of law must be reintroduced into the Church—if the hierarchy is serious (as the pope is) about the Church's orthodoxy. Paul VI was not heeded very well—nor did he do more than state the principles—when he called the crisis after Vatican II a continuation of the Modernist crisis which followed Vatican I. Almost a decade ago he said: "The Catholic Church, in the past and today, has given and gives so much importance to the scrupulous preservation of the authentic revelation. She considers it an inevitable treasure, and is sternly aware of her fundamental duty to defend and transmit the doctrine of the faith in unequivocal terms. Orthodoxy is her first concern" (English *L'Osservatore Romano*, 27 January 1972, p. 1).

It is clear that John Paul II intends to do more than state principles. Dissidents have also made it clear (long before the present pope) that they will fight any law enforcement measures taken to impede their deviance or to break their hold on Catholic institutions. "Betrayal of Vatican II", "un-ecumenical", "purge", "repression" are among the milder descriptions of disciplinary measures. They are correct however, in judging the difficulties faced by John Paul, even if he enjoyed reinforcement of his policies by bishops. A massive effort to enforce Catholic law at this time and at all points would mean repression—or schism, with civil courts asked to adjudicate important aspects of this religious conflict. What then can be done? How should the bishops of the United States support the obvious policies of the Pope? How must they deal with Rome's concern of several years standing that an emerging American Church is in the offing—one likely to create as much trouble for Catholicism as French Gallicanism did for several centuries prior to Vatican I.

Gallicanists demanded the autonomy of the French Church and the right of French bishops to veto Rome's declarations. Americanism, on the other hand, was once thought to be a phantom heresy—to exist only in traditional European minds, not in the United States. On January 22, 1899 Pope Leo XIII expressed concern in his famous letter *Testem Benevolantiae,* in which he excluded from condemnation the legitimate use of the word to signify "the characteristic qualities which reflect honor on the people of America." What Leo XIII considered to be a censurable type of Americanism were the following five specific errors: (1) rejection of external spiritual direction as no longer necessary; (2) extolling natural over supernatural virtues; (3) the preference for active over passive virtues; (4) the rejection of religious vows as incompatible with Christian liberty; (5) a new method of apologetics which would involve certain accommodations with Protestants. Even though these "errors" were not commonplace in the United States at the turn of the Century, certain illicit accommodations with modernity are widely accepted today as characteristics of the future Catholicism. How will the American bishops deal with the situation, if John Paul II pursues the issue further than Leo XIII did eighty years ago?

Presuming that the body of American bishops are one with the pope, their proper course is imitation on the local scene of what they see John Paul II doing universally. Whether the majority of bishops have the same charisms, determation, or leadership qualities of the pope is still to be decided. Even so, the first requirement for the follow-through is a re-awakened sense of who bishops are. They are the heads of the Church. As surely alone as Christ on the Cross, or Peter on his, they stand alone. Therefore, guilt about being men of authority must give way to respect for the responsibility of office. They are being told not to be "triumphal", but the word triumph only means success, not hauteur, not arrogance, not vanity, not autocracy. Few bishops of old were the contemptible people they are sometimes depicted by gossipy historians. The Council quite properly spoke of the Church—and a fortiori the bishop—as pilgrim, but this does not mean he need be subservient to the people in his charge.

The Catholic bishop by definition is neither a chairman of a board nor a titular head, nor a facilitator, nor a mere symbol of the Church's unity. He maintains unity, defends it, forges it, if necessary, by playing the triple role of priest, prophet, king. He may not be good in all roles but as the only father of the Catholic family, he is the final decision-maker, the final law-maker, and the last judge of things Catholic. Unlike the civilian politician he cannot credit or blame another branch of government for his successes and failures. In human terms (and saving God's providence or grace) the prosperity of the Church or its depression depends in the last analysis on the Catholic bishop.

When after the recent papal visit one of Iowa's ministers told a Catholic friend: "You sure have a Pope who knows how to pope.", he clearly envied a Catholic churchman who does well what he is supposed to do. That Protestant cleric would also likely be impressed by a bishop who knows how to bishop. In the interest of good bishopping the question might be asked, therefore: What priorities ought bishops set for themselves? Every bishop will decide his own, of course, but four call for bishops' attention at this particular time:

1 . *Restore priestly and religious life to Catholic standards.*
2. *Place Catholic institutions in the hands of those who will manage them in accordance with the magisterium.*
3. *Reassert their proper role in governance of Catholic institutions of higher learning.*
4. *Reassert their role as chief teachers of and the first defenders of the Catholic faith.*

1. Priestly and Religious Life

Once upon a time self-discipline among priests was taken for granted. So was priestly solidarity with their bishop, and fraternal correction of the priest by the bishop when that was necessary. Discipline of this kind is one of the Church's present needs because the rule now prevalent in many dioceses is *laissez faire.* Obedience is no longer obedience, but a word signifying approval of the superior for what one wants to do or what pleases one to do.

A little respected element of Church law governing priestly life is *canonical mission.* Holy orders of itself does not confer upon a priest a position of authority in the Church, not even the right to preach and teach. Each priest shares in the priesthood of the bishop; he needs jurisdiction to function, either from the local bishop or the bishop of Rome. Canonical mission became a routine matter, to which little thought has been given in recent years, because the priests who received it automatically after ordination had been carefully selected and highly disciplined. Even in those circumstances faculties were denied or withdrawn whenever the public good of the Church made this necessary. Canonical mission no longer ought to be granted compulsively—and must be withdrawn as necessary—because today's bishop, who alone issues faculties, is the sole guarantor of the Church's integrity, which he must not permit priests to dishonor by false life or false teaching.

The same reexamination of a modern bishop's relationship with religious communities is in order. In more peaceful days religious communities were the bishops' specialists. Whether chartered by the Holy See or the local ordinary, they worked for the bishop with remarkable fidelity and achievement. They were rewarded with a mystique and a charism unacknowledged in secular priests and with a freedom to expand their apostolates at will. They were also rewarded with an abundance of postulants and novices. Probably the greatest scandal of the post-Vatican II Church is the animosity of religious communities toward hierarchy and the public misbehavior of their constituents, with bishops usually looking the other way. Outside of the liturgy there are few areas of Church activity to which the Holy See has devoted so much attention and with so little help from American bishops—as the conduct of religious communities. That trend must be reversed through the close cooperation of bishops with Rome, if the faithful are not to be scandalized still further.

This brings us naturally to the Church's institutions which form and mould the priests and religious who edify or scandalize believers.

2. *Catholic Institutions*

The question for bishops is this: What are you going to do to close the gap between the magisterium and Catholic public opinion which results from the direct influence of dissenters in Catholic institutions?

Most fair-minded Protestants would admit that Catholic institutions should not be used to undermine the integrity of Catholic doctrine or the common welfare of the Church. Secular institutions, even the most dramatic, do not permit their staffs to undermine what their constitution require them to do. When undermining occurs in the Church, it usually is the result of acts by Catholic officials, mostly priests or religious, who come under the jurisdiction of bishops. Only bishops can be blamed, if dissenters function within the bishop's household or are protected by them. Bishops usually enforce new directives against priests who refuse to accept the new liturgy, parish councils or accountability procedures. They should also take steps to satisfy complaint of nuns against religious superiors who refuse to grant professed sisters their rights guaranteed under Rome's new decrees on religious life.

But what about the bishop who brings into his diocese a theologian (e.g. Richard McBrien) to tell religious educators that the hierarchy's veto power over Church policy could be overridden in the 1980's by lay councils? What about the bishop who brings Sr. Theresa Kane into his cathedral hall to lecture on the scandalous behavior of the Church toward women? What about the bishop whose diocesan newspaper, or religious education office or whose seminary is staffed with carping critics of Church authority or dissenters who regularly undercut the official teaching of the Church? What about the bishop who knows of serious violations of liturgical norms concerning the most sacred aspects of the Mass itself, and does nothing about it?

On the national level, what about the pressures brought by an overgrown and over-influential USCC bureaucracy against legitimate apostolic enterprise by dedicated Catholics? In recent years USCC has not been over-identified with Catholic movements dubbed "conservative" by the press, although by definition these organizations are defenders of the Church's faith. A new case in point is the USCC reaction to the success of an obscure nun in Birmingham, Alabama in obtaining the first FCC license by a Catholic to a TV satellite. (She is at least a year ahead of the USCC.) Mother Angelica, a Franciscan contemplative, has achieved the relatively impossible, the right to broadcast religious programs via cable television throughout the length and breadth of the United States. *The Florida Catholic* of the Orlando diocese (12 June 1981) reports one USCC official denigrating the Alabama nun calling her "too conservative." The fact that Silvio Cardinal Oddi, Rome's prefect for catechetics, blessed Mother Angelica's "dish" did not prevent another USCC critic (who preferred to remain anonymous) from saying: "Cloistered nuns should stay in their monasteries and not get involved in stuff like this (satellite communications)." The USCC aide apparently does not know that an earlier Franciscan nun (St. Clare) is the patroness of television (proclaimed so by Pius XII a quarter of a century ago). The fact that an enterprising nun intent on preaching Christ's gospel (and doing it with unique talent) must defend herself against bishops' Washington representatives is one sign that all is not well with the Church machinery.

The list of complaints is long and more than peccadillos are involved. Nor are the accusers to be put down as right wing fanatics or bitter traditionalists. An evening conversation with any normal group of 50-year-old-parents of 10-22-year-old children or with the healthy males and females who leave seminaries and novitiates (or change their minds about entering) should satisfy the most complacent observer that the institutional situation of the Church is not good. Two anti-institutional movements of secular society (both closely related) are now sufficiently imbedded into the body of the Church so as to cause long-range trouble—i.e. women's liberation and 'gay' activism. Nuns waging war on a male hierarchy for purely secular purposes and the growing menace of homosexual activists in seminaries do not bode well for the future Church. What is more ominous is the tendency of religious superiors and bishops to be annoyed at those who make the critical reports, not at offenders of moral and canon law. There is a great deal awry when a seminarian-to-be writes about a diocesan official who considers stress on sacraments is out of place in a candidate for the modern priesthood, that commitment to penance and mortification is a possible source of masochism. The practice of turning religious houses into therapy or encounter centers is quite common. In such places intellectual and spiritual formation takes second place. Bishops' decrees count for naught when a respected young ex-religious can write about his experience with a major community: "I believe that the system is deliberately geared to weed out young men who earnestly desire to become churchmen, whose minds and hearts are in conformity with the magisterium and the tradition of Catholicism." If these things are said once, it is once too often. The trouble is that they are being said by many responsible persons living in a wide variety of ecclesiastical circumstances.

When corruption in money matters becomes a matter of public notice, house cleaning is required either by governmental or corporation officials. When the corruption in the Church life is moral and religious, religious superiors first, but bishops eventually, have responsibility to take corrective action. A matter of first priority for contemporary bishops of many dioceses and for the NCCB where its jurisdiction covers the malpractices, is an overhaul of staff. This may be especially true of the USCC machinery which manages repeatedly to turn out drafts of documents which are returned for doctrinal insufficiency, rewritten or scrapped. Continued aberrations of this kind are inexcusable.

3. *Catholic Colleges and Universities*

Archbishop Fulton Sheen, one Wednesday in November, 1972, stood in the rear of the new papal assembly hall, half-listening to Paul VI during a general audience. He was simultaneously holding conversations with American delegates to the Second Congress of Catholic Universities then in session upstairs. Later, as the Pope, upon completion of his address to the pilgrims, was being carried out of the hall, Sheen turned to the American educators and said: "I tell my relatives and friends with college age children to send them to secular colleges where they will have to fight for their faith, rather than to Catholic colleges where it will be taken from them."

This bishop who spent half of his priesthood at the Catholic University of America was distressed, like parents and pastors, by the alarming results of a liberated Catholic college education. Both *The Catholic University in the Modern World* (a 1972 document from that Congress) and *Sapientia Christiana* (1979) assign bishops and/or the Holy See special responsibility for the Catholicity of the institutions and the orthodoxy of the teaching. Catholic higher education officials, with an assist from individual bishops and the USCC, have almost entirely abandoned its juridical ties to the Church, the end result of which has been the teaching of false doctrine on a national scale. Cardinal Newman predicted that a Catholic university would become the Church's rival if the Church was not directly and actively involved in its conduct. (*Idea of a University*, Discourse IX) This prediction is verifiable in the U.S. with Catholic universities and colleges educating increasing numbers of Catholic young in ways inconsistent with their specific reason for existence. Without a reversal of this secularizing trend, initiated belatedly by bishops, the future of the Catholic Church (as hierarchy continues to define it) is clouded in doubt. Both the 1972 and 1979 documents confer on bishops specific authority which up to now they refuse to exercise. It is unconscionable that parents and college youth patronize a college in the assumption that it is Catholic, that it is deepening faith in the Church, that it is forming a wholesome spiritual life, when it is not doing any of these things, while the bishop remains silent or even gives aid and support to the institution.

4. Catholic Faith

The *imprimatur* (let it be printed), the *nihil obstat* (nothing interferes), the *imprimi potest* (it can be printed) were inventions of the Church to protect the faith from the spread of error. Such impressions at a book's beginning were not seals of approval on the content but simply an official indication that the content of the book was not opposed to Catholic doctrine. Most authors found diocesan censors helpful and, prior to Vatican II, the faith of the faithful was protected without recourse to large scale doctrinal investigations or heresy trials. These precautions at the diocesan level, ensured that complaints of false teaching made to Rome were (by recent standards) comparatively few.

On March 7, 1975 the Congregation for the Doctrine of the Faith liberalized Church procedures for the censorship of books. The Bible, liturgical and catechetical books were still required to have ecclesiastical approval. However, books on scripture, theology, canon law etc. needed the *imprimatur* only if they were to be used as teaching texts in Church institutions. In all other cases, books on these and other Catholic subjects did not require an *imprimatur*, although it was recommended. Books sold or distributed in Churches also were expected to have an *imprimatur*.

These relaxed regulations have led to the proliferations of Catholic books at odds with Church teaching. Not only are books and magazines liberally sold and distributed in Churches without the *im-*

primatur, but religious communities (the Paulist and Claretian Fathers, especially) regularly publish books which contain matters contrary to faith and morals. Furthermore, books without an *imprimatur* (e.g. Avery Dulles' *Models of the Church*) are used *de facto* as texts in college classrooms and diocesan institutes. Finally, some books carry a bishop's *imprimatur* which actually contravene Catholic doctrine (Philip Keane's *Sexual Morality* is a classic case). Some books obtain an *imprimatur* although omitting certain aspects of Catholic doctrine, e.g. Mass as sacrifice, original sin, the possibility of actual sin, the commandments etc. The excuses offered in justification of this practice are many. Even where the denial of Catholic doctrine is not intended or implied (and intelligent readers readily sense the message), the end result is a distorted view of Catholic doctrine presented to readers, frequently to children.

If bishops do not tighten their own procedures in this important aspect of faith-protection, one can only anticipate the further contamination of the faithful and belated actions by the Holy See. The Australian bishops, for example, have no hesitancy in dealing with books which may endanger the faith. Almost as soon as Richard McBrien's *Catholicism* was published in their country, they issued a statement giving reasons for disapproval and concluded with the following warning: "We do not recommend it to the ordinary layman or laywoman as a book in which to look up some point of Catholic teaching. Even more we do not regard it as a reliable book to place in the hands of senior students in secondary schools" (*The Catholic Leader* [Brisbane] 7 September 1980). Although *Catholicism,* an American book by a Hartford priest, is being used in Catholic colleges of the United States as a text and without an *imprimatur,* no similar guidance has been given to American Catholics. To the contrary, the book is being widely praised in reviews and is used in Catholic college classrooms without serious contradiction from American bishops.

Perhaps the time has come to recognize the battle for the Church for what it is—a power struggle between irreconcilable forces within the Church, whose outcome will be decided by those who have superior weaponry and use it. Most Catholics, especially bishops, do not like to frame the contest in these terms. A battle of ideas, perhaps, a transitional period customary after every ecumenical council, resistance of the new by the old, excessive experimentation with the old by the new, immanentism versus transcendentalism, sectarianism against ecumenism, and so forth—anything but what it now is, a fight to decide who runs the Church. What the Church stands for no longer seems to be a matter of grave concern to the parties on either side of the ideological spectrum—be they bishops or dissenters. It is now commonplace for people to 'do their own thing' in conformity to old or new standards, as they wish. The only matter remaining to be decided is—which Catholicism will be institutionalized? And this will be decided only by the victors in the present power struggle.

The days of Henri de Lubac, Yves Conger, Karl Rahner, and John Courtney Murray versus the Cardinal Ottavianis of the Church, or the Cardinal McIntyres, are over. Now we are engaged in a great ecclesiastical war to test whether this Catholic Church or any Christian Church, so conceived by Christ and so dedicated to his purposes, can long endure. The antagonists are John Paul II and bishops committed to their understanding of Vatican II and a warring intellectual elite that now includes, among others, the Hans Kungs, Gregory Baums, Charles Currans, Edward Schillebeeckxs. Also involved are the public relations' voices for this cause—the Francis X. Murphys and Richard McBriens, who talk power and resistance to power more than they talk about faith or holiness. Whether it be academic light bearers who attend Vatican III conferences at Notre Dame University, religious community leaders defying Rome's degrees, Andrew Greeley using the diocesan press to promote "communal Catholicism" or Msgr. John Egan's "Parish Corporate Renewal Network", the end result is the same—the end of the hierarchic church.

Is this an extreme assessment of the Church? Listen to feminist theologian Rosemary Radford Reuther who graces many a lectern in well-known Catholic campus halls and convents. In her view the gap between the Church's pastoral life and the "revolutionary theological implications" of Vatican II is a major religious problem—not of modernism versus Catholicism, but "a problem of ecclesiastical power structures." The Council called for collegiality, she insists correctly, but the hierarchy combats democratization and subverts the authority of the new theology. Here is how she sees the burning issue:

> A new consensus could only come about if this traditional power could be deposed and the Church restructured on conciliar, democratic lines accountable to the people. Then the theological consensus of the academy could serve as a guide for the pastoral teaching of the Church. This is really what Kung is calling for: that the academy replace the hierarchy as the teaching magisterium of the Church. This cannot be accomplished by the academy itself. It entails the equivalent of the French Revolution in the Church, the deposing of a monarchical for a democratic constitution of the Church. No one has seriously discussed how this is to be done. But one thing is sure. It will not be legislated by the present power holders. It demands a revolution from below of a type that is difficult to imagine, much less to organize. (*Journal of Ecumenical Studies*, Winter 1980, p. 65).

Recognizing that the theological split between the academy and the hierarchy makes voluntary consensus impossible, "the best we can hope for is the defense of pluralism." Curialists will not recognize it but "pluralism can be defended only by making sure that this hierarchical power structure is not strong enough to repress successfully the independent institutional bases of conciliar and liberation theology." Reuther quite correctly measures the institutional bases of the new theologies.

> These are Catholic academic institutions, Catholic faculties of theology at colleges and universities, seminaries (primarily order rather than diocesan seminaries), renewed religious orders, independent study and action centers and movements concerned with social justice, and the independent Catholic media. The reason why there is any significant intellectual pluralism in the Catholic Church today is primarily because the hierarchy has lost control of a number of important institutions and the Catholic media. In addition, new kinds of Catholic movements have developed outside of direct ecclesiastical control. These are the social basis of liberal and liberationist theology. (*Ibid*, p. 66).

That is a fair estimation of the present situation, one for which she is grateful because she recognizes that the formidable power of John Paul II may frustrate what looks to her like the inevitable victory of her libertarian troops. She anticipates "a concerted effort by the Vatican and national hierarchies to recapture control over these Catholic groups, especially educational institutions and religious orders and to marginalize and delegitimize the catholicity of those autonomous lay movements, action centers, and media which they cannot control." The defenders of theological pluralism in the Church are not without weapons, however; they have government money instead of Church money to keep the Catholic University of America independent of bishops, can use the American Association of University Professors against Church authority if it dares to infringe on academic freedom (even of priests who marry) and will exercise constant vigilance against the internalization of unjust power within the Church. Reuther provides this final piece of advice: "If, as I contend, the lack of consensus in theology is rooted in power struggle, then the liberal wing of this dissension must defend the autonomy and Catholicity of its institutional power bases, if it hopes to survive as an option for the future" (ibid, p. 67). She wants the continuation of what she unashamedly calls "internal schism", the kind that still plagues the Dutch Church in spite of John Paul II.

Whatever one thinks of Rosemary Reuther's opinions of the faith and Church, her political judgments about the contemporary Catholic problematic are verified almost every time prominent Catholic dissenters write against the magisterium or position themselves against any effort by Church authority to re-institutionalize its own ortho- doxy. The revolutionary or schismatic significance of their activity becomes manifest in the tone or content of what they say and do.

Consider now the well-matured views of Richard McCormick, Avery Dulles, and Raymond E. Brown, all of whom have held and occa- sionally still hold high places in the councils of American bishops. The March 1981 issue of *Theological Studies* illustrates how far all three have departed from their "tentative", "interim", and "centrist" theological "probings" of years ago. Each of these authors still uses these terms as if their present views are still experimental hypotheses seeking developed understanding of the faith, when in fact all three now hold hardened positions *against* what Church officials are saying in their formal pronouncements and catechetical directories.

Apart from the fact that McCormick's careful phrasings about moral matters are hardly more than utilitarian rationalizations for actions condemned by the Church as immoral, the Jesuit moralist goes beyond organizing theologians against bishops. He would now inspire bishops to oppose the pope. McCormick today thinks that cooperation by theologians in dialogue with bishops is vain—(his word is "nugatory")—"if the bishops do not speak their true mind after such cooperation has occurred" (ibid, p. 117). Presumptively, bishops agree with him and not the Pope but are cowardly about expressing their new convictions. In his *Fifth Synod of Bishops* (1980) on family mat- ters, McCormick, by carefully assembling dissenting authors, makes it clear that he wants bishops and pastors to fight the pope as freely as theologians now do. Then remembering that pastors function as preachers and teachers in the Church not by virtue of their orders but under the jurisdictions of Catholic law, McCormick turns to Avery Dulles to "prove" that scholarly clerics do not need canonical mission to publicize their theological theories about Catholic doctrine. Peer approval alone is all that is required. Assuming as a fact and as a solid Catholic principle that two conflicting magisteria may legitimately co- exist in the Church—each soliciting their own following among the faithful—McCormick sees only one obstacle to be overcome for his (and Dulles') views to dominate—viz., the suppression of "the third magisterium" i.e. "simple and devout believers (and their theological supporters) who have not been trained to distinguish the deposit of faith from traditional formulations" (*Fifth Synod of Bishops,* p. 118). McCormick surely knows this last statement to be untrue, but as the newcomer to the theological disputes he has helped proliferate, he is frustrated by his inability to persuade the hierarchy, large segments of the worldwide theological community (which he rarely cites) and the faithful that the "new morality", of which he is now the premier defender, is really Christian. Yet McCormick relentlessly pursues his objective of undermining traditional Christian moral positions by appealing (through the voice of Karl Rahner) to the magisterium's toleration after *Humanae Vitae* of the massive assault on the magisterium as evidence that authoritative statements even of Vatican II (e.g. *Lumen Gentium* No. 25) do not always have binding force on the Christian conscience (ibid, p. 79). Factually, Church authority has in many instances for good and bad reasons tolerated moral evils and heresies for centuries before finally rooting them out of the Church body.

Fr. Raymond Brown's article, "Scripture as the Word of God," in the same issue of *Theological Studies* makes it impossible for a Christian reader to assert with confidence that he can find in the Bible any so-called "word" of God that he can be sure is "God's" word. Brown may fully accept, as he says (*Theological Studies,* March 1981, p. 4), "the Roman Catholic doctrine of the Bible as the word of God", but it is difficult for an open-minded reader of this article to be sure after reading it just where that word would be found. Brown compiles a long list of places where the word of God may not be found—neither in the Wisdom books, nor in the Psalms, nor in the Prophets and Moses, not even in the "sayings of Jesus" which often are "Church-foundational", not words of Jesus at all. Says Brown: "Although theoretically these words were spoken in the early 30's, often there is little evidence that they influenced Church life in the next few decades" (ibid, p. 12). If the believer at a loss with the Bible thinks he can then turn to the Church to discover there whatever simple word of God might ever have been contained in scripture, he will learn from Brown that it is not possible to accept the stated Church view that the Bible was inspired of God and inerrant. Brown puzzles why our own "insecurity" keeps pushing us to look for "absolute answers" in our search for biblical meaning. The Brown Bible is a very different book from what "Catholics who have little knowledge of the Bible and make simple assumptions" believe. Brown says: "Whether the words of the Bible reflect revelation received from God or constitute an account inspired by God, they remain very much human words, reflecting partial insight and time conditioned vision" (ibid., p. 18). At best Christians must depend on scripturists to discover what little bit of God's word might be found there. Even then Brown (arguing that he follows Vatican II) thinks the only assumption we can make about the truth contained in the Bible is that "God wants the salvation of His people." (One does not have to be a Christian to accept this minimalist view of Biblical content.)

Brown downgrades all the Church's most solemn statements about scripture, even Vatican II's declaration that "the books of scripture must be acknowledged as teaching firmly, faithfully and without error that truth which God wanted put into the sacred writings for the sake of our salvation." (*Dei Verbum* No. 11) This formula, he says, was merely a "face saving device" to placate conservatives at the Council, but the meaning of the assertion is still ambiguous. Popes are quickly moving toward his views, Brown contends, even as they requote "with praise" past papal statements which they no longer believe to be true. If Brown were correct there would be little true in which popes or people can believe with certainty about the supposed revelation on which the Church's divine claims are based. In a real sense, therefore, Brown is a far more radical reinterpreter of the Christian meaning than McCormick. But, like the Jesuit moralist, the Sulpician biblicist bases the correctness of his new interpretations by pointing to what, in comparison to forty years ago, the present day Church authorities tolerate from their own world of biblical scholarship (ibid., p. 16).

Such "doubt, hesitation, search" no matter how camouflaged by an ironic tone or copious footnotes, translates into Rosemary Reuther's "internal schism" among other scholars, among priests, among religious and the faithful. For example, Jesuit Joseph A. O'Hare, *America's* editor, writing for the Claretian Fathers in *U.S. Catholic* (April 1981, pp. 41-44), is happy at the thought of a future Catholicism composed of "communal Catholics"—i.e. those who "would exercise selective obedience to the Church authority." In order for Vatican II's Christian renewal to move forward in the United States it is important, thinks O'Hare, for American Catholics to get rid of their unfortunate legacy of "popolatry", that excessive reverence for the pope which blinds them to the wrinkles, flaws, and fallibility of much of what he (and all Church authority) does.

Demythologization of scripture and Christ and disestablishment of the pope has been going on for such a long time in Catholic circles that its message is now deeply rooted in the psyches of Churchgoers—particularly the young. The Third National Conference of Catholic Student Leaders held at the Catholic University of America, February 19-22, 1981, shows how far undergraduates from such Catholic colleges as Villanova, Notre Dame and Scranton have come from the days when such students were exemplars of adherence to Catholicism's faith and policies. Now—in a report prepared by Jeffrey D. Lynch, the conference coordinator—they make it clear (1) that their decision to attend a Catholic college was not based on its "Catholic-ness"; (2) they "must challenge what they are being taught in the classroom, especially the Catholic/Christian foundation of their religious value system"; (3) that after the first semester they "should be able to choose whatever living arrangements which suit them best", a reference to the effort of Catholic colleges historically to prevent cohabitation of the sexes on or near their campuses.

The 1981 convention of the National Catholic Educational Association in New York City heard news from William McCready that more than eighty percent of young Catholics reject the teaching of the Church on sexual matters and almost as many reject the infallibility of the Pope. Only thirty-seven percent of the young attend Mass weekly, his report said, with Catholic education itself no guarantee of full acceptance by its students of Catholic doctrine. This represents an almost complete reversal of young Catholic behavioral response in a single generation. What is also no longer surprising is how important Catholic educators questioned on the statistics agree that dissent to Church teaching by Catholic youth is healthy. Fr. John F. Meyers, NCEA president, considered it proper for Catholic schools to teach dissent. One school superintendent explained the weakened allegiance with the observation that Catholic school teachers no longer require students "to swallow hook, line and sinker everything presented to them." Fr. Andrew Greeley said you do not have to accept the whole picture to be a good Catholic (*New York Daily News*, 23 April 1981, p. 22).

One wonders—on this basis—why the Catholic Church keeps these schools open? Certainly contemporary Catholic educators who detach themselves so completely from the religious results of their effort (as their predecessors did not) would be held to greater account, if not dismissed from their posts, if the scores on secular learning in their schools were equally low.

At the 1981 convention, NCEA gave Raymond E. Brown another opportunity to usurp "the center" of the Church for himself and the religious educators who relativize Catholic doctrinal positions while absolutizing 'Church-in-process'. Fr. Brown among others is frequently cited as justification for their selective adherence to things Catholic. If Fr. Brown's thinking represents "the center" of the Church what are all the recent Popes going back to John XXIII complaining about? Why was Paul VI in the last years of his life lecturing bishops on orthodoxy and their responsibility to teach and defend it? Why is John Paul II going directly to the people and to bishops with the authentic Catholic message that makes some NCEA speakers uneasy?

As the national representatives of Catholicism, the body of bishops continue to ignore this situation to the peril of the Church. Bishops have attempted to co-opt their ideological enemies in the expectation that it could bridge the doctrinal chasm with a new consensus mediated by hierarchy. That is not happening nor is it likely to happen on terms acceptable to the magisterium. Will bishops now accept Reuther's judgment that only unconditional surrender by the hierarchy is the goal of doctrinal liberationists? Can they understand that so-called pluralism is only the scholars' way station to an un-Catholic end? Or do enough bishops today believe that *orthopraxis* is the better "rule of faith" than orthodoxy?

That bishops are now an important part of the Catholic problem is only too evident.

The Final Word

It is a common complaint of many twentieth century scholars that advanced thinkers often are oppressed by Church authority. They make many references also to the modern errors of the magisterium and offer evidence of how Catholicism is embarrassed whenever bishops are forced to catch-up with thinkers who frequently are compelled to do their thinking under an ecclesiastical cloud. These complaints, of course, are one-sided judgments of complicated Church situations, which ignore the fact that hierarchy is not called upon to do advanced thinking but to protect the faith against any public effort which would dilute or deny the meaning or content of revelation. Advanced thinking is not necessarily Catholic thinking.

A better case can be made for the exercise of the magisterium in modern times. Pius IX properly saw secularism and scientism as threats to religion a century before their full effects were noticeable in society. Pius X identified modernism for what it was, long before unbelieving and half-believing intellectuals had any power to corrupt the faith of church-goers. Pope Pius XII prophetically anticipated that the misuse of the scholarly enterprise, especially in scriptural matters, would adversely affect the religious practice of the faithful. In between, Leo XIII was describing the evils of capitalism as a warning to Christians enamored of its money-making possibilities. Pius XI's analysis of Marxism is still a classic warning of today's Catholic religious who find Communism the answer to the poverty of the Third World. Paul VI's *Humanae Vitae* has not achieved the respect it deserves for its analysis of the moral evils eroding the vitality of the Christian family and society itself. But give it time.

John Paul II looks more charismatic than any of these popes, and just as knowledgeable as Leo XIII and Pius XII. But neither his photogenetic qualities, nor his charm, nor his intellect are the answer to the Church's contemporary problem. Who he is in the Church and who bishops are ought to be key elements of any answer. Here is how the present pope defined the issue for the American bishops in his meeting with them on October 5, 1979:

> Because of my personal responsibility, and because of our common
> pastoral responsibility for the people of God in the United States, I desire
> to strengthen you in your individual and joint pastoral activities by en-
> couraging you to stand fast in the holiness and truth of our Lord Jesus
> Christ. And in you I desire to honor Jesus Christ, the Shepherd and
> Bishop of souls. Because we have been called to be shepherds of the
> flock, we realize that we must present ourselves as humble servants of the
> Gospel. Our leadership will be effective only to the extent that our own
> discipline is genuine.

Bibliography

Baum, Gregory. *Religion and Alienation,* New York: Paulist Press, 1975.

Bouyer, Louis. *The Decomposition of Catholicism,* Chicago: Franciscan Herald Press, 1969.

Brown, Raymond. *Crises Facing the Church,* 1975, New York: Paulist Press, 1975.

Castelli, James. *What the Church is Doing for Divorced and Remarried Catholics,* Chicago: Claretian Fathers Booklet, 1979.

Curran, Charles. *Contraception: Authority and Dissent,* New York: Herder & Herder, 1969.

DeLubac, Henri. *Splendour of the Church,* New York: Sheed & Ward, 1956.

Fracchia, Charles. *Second Spring,* New York: Harper & Row, 1980.

Goddijn, Walter. *Deffered Revolution,* Amsterdam: Elsevier, 1975.

Greeley, Andrew. *The Making of the Popes,* Kansas City, Kansas: Andrews & McNeel, 1979.

Hebblethwaite, Peter. *The Runaway Church,* New York: The Seabury Press, 1975.

Keane, Philip. *Sexual Morality: A Catholic Perspective,* New York: Paulist Press, 1977.

Kelly, George A. *The Battle for the American Church,* New York: Doubleday and Co., 1979.

Kennedy, Eugene. *The New Sexuality,* New York: Doubleday, 1973.

Kosnik, Anthony, et al. *Human Sexuality,* New York: Paulist Press, 1977.

Kung, Hans. *On Being a Christian,* New York: Doubleday, 1976.

Lindbeck, George, et al. *University Divinity Schools,* New York: The Rockefeller Foundation, March, 1976.

McBrien, Richard. *American Catholicism,* Oak Grove, Michigan: Winston Press, 1980.

McKenzie, John. *The Old Testament Without Illusions,* Chicago: Thomas More Press, 1979.

Murphy, Francis X. *Catholic Perspectives on Population Issues,* Population Reference Bureau, February, 1981.

Santayana, George. *The Winds of Doctrine,* New York: Dent, 1913.

Schillebeeckx, Edward. *Ministry,* New York: Crossroads, 1981.

Studies in the Spirituality of Jesuits, Vol. IX, January-March, 1977 St. Louis University.

Tracy, David. *Blessed Rage for Order,* New York: Seabury Press, 1975.

_____, et. al. *Toward Vatican III,* New York: Seabury Press, 1978.

Index